Incredible—
but TR

D0356514

Robert Ripley and his staff have traveled to the farthest corners of the world in their continuing search for extraordinary facts. This collection of inconceivable feats, wonderous sights, and apparent miracles is sure to convince you that **truth is indeed stranger than fiction.**

Ripley's—·Believe It or Not!
17th Series
is an original POCKET BOOK edition.

Ripley's Believe It or Not! titles

Ripley's Believe It or Not! 2nd Series
Ripley's Believe It or Not! 3rd Series
Ripley's Believe It or Not! 4th Series
Ripley's Believe It or Not! 5th Series
Ripley's Believe It or Not! 7th Series
Ripley's Believe It or Not! 8th Series
Ripley's Believe It or Not! 9th Series
Ripley's Believe It or Not! 10th Series
Ripley's Believe It or Not! 11th Series
Ripley's Believe It or Not! 12th Series
Ripley's Believe It or Not! 13th Series
Ripley's Believe It or Not! 14th Series
Ripley's Believe It or Not! 15th Series
Ripley's Believe It or Not! 16th Series
Ripley's Believe It or Not! 17th Series
Ripley's Believe It or Not! 18th Series
Ripley's Believe It or Not! 19th Series
Ripley's Believe It or Not! 20th Series
Ripley's Believe It or Not! 21st Series
Ripley's Believe It or Not! 22nd Series
Ripley's Believe It or Not! 23rd Series
Ripley's Believe It or Not! Anniversary Edition
The Best of 50 Years of Ripley's Believe It or Not!

Published by POCKET BOOKS

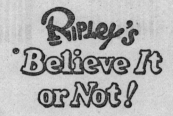

Ripley's Believe It or Not!

17th Series

PUBLISHED BY POCKET BOOKS NEW YORK

RIPLEY'S BELIEVE IT OR NOT!® 17th SERIES

POCKET BOOK edition published September, 1971
8th printing .... June, 1975

This original POCKET BOOK edition is printed from brand-new plates made from newly set, clear, easy-to-read type.
POCKET BOOK editions are published by POCKET BOOKS, a division of Simon & Schuster, Inc., 630 Fifth Avenue, New York, N.Y. 10020. Trademarks registered in the United States and other countries.

We are now dealing with *Ripley's Believe It or Not! 17th Series*. Since seventeen was bound to come up in the course of time, we did our research early and have come up with the following "Believe It or Nots" on the subject.

First on our list is Nakaeia, Chief of the island of Butaritari, one of the Gilbert group on the equator in the Pacific. He was the husband of seventeen wives and the spirit of free enterprise stirred mightily within his breast. He regularly hired out his seventeen wives as building laborers to private contractors, and pocketed their earnings.

Next on the list is a Spanish knight named Aldano Rojas who saved the life of King Philip II of Spain before he ascended the throne. Many years later Rojas was asked what boon he would consider adequate as a reward for his deed. He said that he would like to make the number "Diez y siete" (seventeen) a part of his family name. The reason was that he had wooed and married a young lady named Eulalia, who was only seventeen to Rojas's fifty-two, and he wanted this lucky fact commemorated to the end of time. Eulalia had been his son's fiancée but when the young man died in a duel, the young lady transferred her affections to her former prospective father-in-law.

In 1912 an American named Shueck applied to a judge in Seattle for a change of name. He wanted his name changed to "Seventeen". The reporters got busy on this request and discovered that Shueck was riding in a streetcar when Orville Wright had piloted the first heavier-than-air machine at Kitty Hawk, N.C., on December 17, 1903. Because like many Americans he had paid slight attention to what he saw, he wanted the date belatedly made part of his family name.

I have no more "Believe It or Nots" on the number seventeen, but let the above serve as an introduction to a new work filled to overflowing with the most exquisite incredibilities accumulated as in a treasure trove in the BELIEVE IT OR NOT! archives. As the book takes wing, it will dazzle and delight you with its hundreds of illustrations and the marvels of its "Believe It or Not" assertions.

This writer is proud that all the items in this new book have been researched and endorsed by him, while the artwork has been supervised by the distinguished Art Director, Paul Frehm.

—Norbert Pearlroth
Research Director
BELIEVE IT OR NOT!

THE DAILY WORLD in Omaha, Nebr., TO HONOR A VISIT BY PRESIDENT CLEVELAND PRINTED 4 COPIES OF THE NEWSPAPER ON SATIN (October 12, 1887).

EUGENE COQUEBERT de MONTRRET (1785-1849) WAS FOR YEARS OFFICIAL TRANSLATOR FOR THE FRENCH MINISTRY OF FOREIGN AFFAIRS -YET HE WAS DEAF AND MUTE

HE BECAME A DEAF-MUTE AFTER AN ACCIDENT AT THE AGE OF 5, BUT MASTERED 21 LANGUAGES-ALL OF WHICH HE LEARNED TO READ AND WRITE WITHOUT INSTRUCTION

THE ORGAN WITH A HEART THE LEFT PILLAR OF THE ORGAN OF the Jacobi Church, in Stettin, Poland, ENCLOSES A GOLDEN CAPSULE CONTAINING THE HEART OF COMPOSER KARL LOEWE

LOEWE, WHO DIED IN 1869, WAS THE CHURCH ORGANIST FOR 46 YEARS

THE BARN OWL found on the island of Jamaica ALWAYS SWALLOWS MICE, BIRDS, LIZARDS AND FROGS WHOLE -FEATHERS, BONES AND ALL

AN **ANCIENT IVORY SNUFFBOTTLE** WHICH HAS ENGRAVED WITHIN AN AREA OF ONE SQUARE INCH **688 CHINESE CHARACTERS**

MARY KINSMAN of Landaff, N.H.
MADE 5 PATCHWORK QUILTS, EACH CONSISTING OF 599 PIECES, SPUN 100 SKEINS OF YARN, AND KNITTED 22 PAIRS OF MITTENS *-ALL IN HER 81st YEAR*

THE **CHURCH** of Cave, N.Z., WAS BUILT IN 1929 *WITHOUT A SINGLE NAIL AND WITHOUT THE USE OF A HAMMER* ITS WALLS ARE STONE, ITS ROOF SLATE AND ITS WOODEN SEATS WERE HEWN OUT OF SOLID LUMBER WITH AN ADZE

THE HAMMOCK BRIDGES OF SOUTHERN NIGERIA
BRIDGES AS HIGH AS 100 FEET ABOVE RAGING RIVERS ARE BUILT BY JOINING TOGETHER CREEPERS FROM TREES OVERHANGING THE WATER -TO FORM AN OTHERWISE UNSUPPORTED FOOTPATH

FUJIWARA MICHINAGA
(966-1027)
A JAPANESE STATESMAN WAS THE FATHER-IN-LAW OF 3 SUCCESSIVE JAPANESE EMPERORS AND THE GRANDFATHER OF 4 EMPERORS

JOHN M. FLYNN
CAPTAINED A 7-MAN BOWLING TEAM OF NOVICES WHICH WON A NEW ORLEANS SCRATCH LEAGUE CHAMPIONSHIP WITH A FINAL SET IN WHICH THERE WERE NO FOULS, NO MISSES, AND NOT A SINGLE SPLIT

THE HAMSTER
HAS A GESTATION PERIOD OF ONLY 16 DAYS

THE MAN WHO TALKED HIS WAY OFF THE GALLOWS

EDMOND AUGER (1530-1591)
SENTENCED TO BE HANGED DURING
THE FRENCH CIVIL WAR
WAS CLIMBING THE LADDER TO
THE SCAFFOLD WHEN HE WAS ASKED
IF HE HAD A FEW LAST WORDS

CLINGING TO THE LADDER HE MADE
SUCH A MOVING SPEECH THAT HIS
CAPTORS WEPT AND SET HIM FREE

MATHEMATICAL CALCULATIONS
AIMED AT FINDING
THE AREA OF A
CIRCLE —CONTAINED
IN THE RHIND PAPYRUS
WRITTEN IN EGYPT
3,615 YEARS AGO

HOT TYPE
THE EUREKA SENTINEL (Nevada)
WENT TO PRESS AGAIN SO FAST AFTER A
DISASTROUS FIRE SWEPT ITS PLANT THAT THE
BUILDING WAS STILL SMOLDERING, THE PRESSES
WERE RED HOT, AND THE TYPESETTERS HAD
TO BE DOUSED WITH COLD WATER (April, 1879)

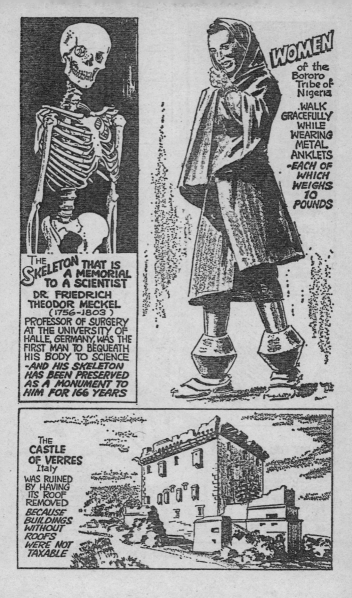

WOMEN of the Bororo Tribe of Nigeria .WALK GRACEFULLY WHILE WEARING METAL ANKLETS -EACH OF WHICH WEIGHS 10 POUNDS

THE *SKELETON* THAT IS A MEMORIAL TO A SCIENTIST
DR. FRIEDRICH THEODOR MECKEL (1756-1803) PROFESSOR OF SURGERY AT THE UNIVERSITY OF HALLE, GERMANY, WAS THE FIRST MAN TO BEQUEATH HIS BODY TO SCIENCE -AND HIS SKELETON HAS BEEN PRESERVED AS A MONUMENT TO HIM FOR 166 YEARS

THE CASTLE OF VERRES Italy WAS RUINED BY HAVING ITS ROOF REMOVED *BECAUSE BUILDINGS WITHOUT ROOFS WERE NOT TAXABLE*

THE **COWFISH** of Ceylon HAS HORNS AND LOOKS REMARKABLY LIKE A COW

HEARTBREAK ALLEY in Tours, France THOSE WHO USED IT AS A LOVERS' LANE WERE SO UNLUCKY THAT *SWEETHEARTS HAVE AVOIDED IT FOR 500 YEARS*

PAINT BRUSHES USED BY MOUNTAIN BUSHMEN OF Basutoland, So. Africa, CONSIST OF BIRD FEATHERS STUCK INTO THE ENDS OF TINY REEDS

SAMUEL L. TILLEY (1818-1896) CANADIAN STATESMAN FIRST SUGGESTED CALLING HIS COUNTRY A "DOMINION" BECAUSE OF AN APT QUOTATION IN THE BIBLE (Psalm 72, Verse 8): *" He shall have dominion from sea to sea and from the river unto the ends of the earth"*

THE MAN WHO WAS KILLED BY A POEM

ROGER ASCHAM (1515-1568) the English poet WORKED SO FEVERISHLY TO COMPOSE A POETIC TRIBUTE IN LATIN TO MARK THE 10th ANNIVERSARY OF THE CORONATION OF QUEEN ELIZABETH I – *THAT HE DIED OF EXHAUSTION*

THE MAGNETIC OBSERVATORY at Trinity College, in Dublin, NOW USED AS A WEATHER BUREAU, WAS BUILT IN 1837 ENTIRELY *WITHOUT THE USE OF IRON*

BLONAY CASTLE – Vaud, Switzerland, OCCUPIED BY THE SAME FAMILY FOR 794 YEARS!

THE SEA RAVEN
A FISH NICKNAMED THE "SALLY GROWLER" BECAUSE *IT EMITS LOUD GRUNTS*

THE WALL OF BONES
THE FINAL RESTING PLACE OF THE DEAD IN SOME PARTS OF SPAIN—IF THEIR KIN CANNOT PAY AN ANNUAL RENTAL FOR STORAGE OF THEIR COFFINS —IS A BONEYARD IN WHICH THE SKULLS AND BONES ARE NEATLY PILED IN LONG ROWS

The TURQUOISE PARROT of Australia

PLACES THE LEAVES OF THE HIGHLY AROMATIC TEA TREE AMONG ITS FEATHERS *TO DRIVE AWAY INSECTS*

REGINA LEININGER
KIDNAPED BY DELAWARE INDIANS AT THE AGE OF 10 DURING THE PENN'S CREEK MASSACRE OF 1755 HAD FORGOTTEN HER NAME AND FAMILY BY THE TIME SHE WAS RESCUED 8 YEARS LATER, BUT RECOGNIZED HER MOTHER *WHEN SHE SANG A HYMN FAMILIAR FROM HER CHILDHOOD*

"Chubby" A HORSE TRAINED BY COWBOY ACTOR FREEMAN CLARK TO ROLLER SKATE

THE SEACOW A FISH FOUND near Tahiti HAS 2 HORNS AND LARGE EYES LIKE A COW

THE VERTICAL VILLAGE OF EL ARBAA Algeria THE 100 HOMES ARE BUILT INTO THE FACE OF A HIGH PRECIPICE —MOST OF THEM ACCESSIBLE ONLY BY LADDERS

CALIPH OMAR I (582-644) of Islam IN A PERIOD OF 29 YEARS CAPTURED 36,000 CASTLES AND FORTRESSES, DESTROYED 4,000 TEMPLES AND CONSTRUCTED 1,400 MOSQUES

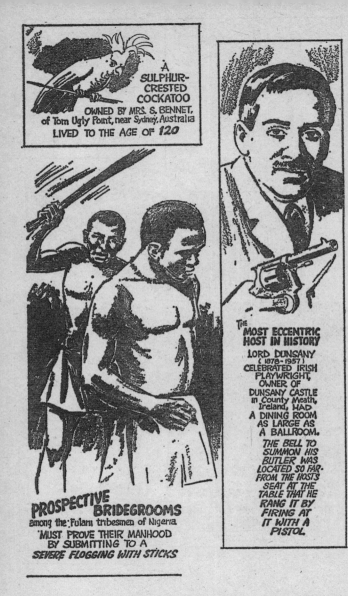

A SULPHUR-CRESTED COCKATOO OWNED BY MRS. S. BENNET, of Tom Ugly Point, near Sydney, Australia LIVED TO THE AGE OF 120

PROSPECTIVE BRIDEGROOMS among the Fulani tribesmen of Nigeria MUST PROVE THEIR MANHOOD BY SUBMITTING TO A SEVERE FLOGGING WITH STICKS

THE MOST ECCENTRIC HOST IN HISTORY LORD DUNSANY (1878-1957) CELEBRATED IRISH PLAYWRIGHT, OWNER OF DUNSANY CASTLE in County Meath, Ireland, HAD A DINING ROOM AS LARGE AS A BALLROOM.

THE BELL TO SUMMON HIS BUTLER WAS LOCATED SO FAR FROM THE HOST'S SEAT AT THE TABLE THAT HE RANG IT BY FIRING AT IT WITH A PISTOL.

ST. ANTHONY'S CHAPEL in Bochnia, Poland, IN WHICH DAILY SERVICES ARE HELD *IS HEWN OUT OF ROCK SALT*

HUGHES BOUFFÉ
(1800–1888)
FRENCH ACTOR AND DIRECTOR FOR 40 YEARS ATE ONLY ONE MEAL A DAY
ALWAYS DINING AT MIDNIGHT ON BEEFSTEW, BOILED BEEF TURNIPS, BEET ROOT AND POTATO SALAD

A **TURKISH MINARET** constructed in Pecs, Hungary, in the 17th century *SERVES TODAY AS THE BELFRY FOR A NEARBY CHURCH*

NATURE'S MOST INHOSPITABLE BIRD
THE GREY LOURIE of Africa UPON SIGHTING A HUMAN DISTINCTLY SCREECHES *"GO AWAY"*

A **WOODEN CROSS** ERECTED IN the Apennine Mountains, near Ospitaletto, Italy, WHERE A VAGRANT DIED IN A BLIZZARD IN 1904, CARRIES THE INSCRIPTION: "To the Unknown Tramp"

HURON and **IROQUOIS INDIANS** AFTER 25 SAILORS IN JACQUES CARTIER'S CREW DIED OF SCURVY IN CANADA IN 1536 SUGGESTED THAT HIS MEN DRINK A MEDICATION MADE BY BOILING THE *LEAVES AND BARK OF A SPRUCE TREE* HUNDREDS OF YEARS LATER SCIENTISTS VERIFIED THAT SCURVY IS CAUSED BY A LACK OF VITAMIN C – WHICH *IS FOUND IN EVERGREENS*

GIOVANNI FRANCESCO CONTI (1486-1567) WROTE POETRY SO SWIFTLY THAT THROUGHOUT THE LAST 25 YEARS OF HIS LIFE *HE TURNED OUT 800 VERSES EACH DAY*

THE **WILD ARGALI** of Asia BECAME THE FIRST DOMESTICATED SHEEP – TAMED MORE THAN 5,000 YEARS AGO

WILLIAM **BACKENSTO** of the University of Toledo, Ohio, LEADING SCORER ON ITS BASKETBALL TEAM, MADE STRAIGHT A's IN CALCULUS, PSYCHOLOGY, ECONOMICS AND POLITICAL SCIENCE BUT IN PHYSICAL EDUCATION HIS GRADE WAS ONLY A B

EARLY MATCH BOXES WERE OFTEN MADE OF WOOD IN THE SHAPE OF A SHOE

THE MYSTERIOUS MEDICINE WHEEL OF THE BIG HORN MOUNTAINS near Lovell, Wyoming THE FORMATION OF STONES EXISTED EVEN BEFORE THE AREA WAS INHABITED BY INDIANS

THE CROWN OF THORNS A MADAGASCAR CACTUS CAN BE TRAINED TO GROW IN A CIRCULAR SHAPE SO IT CAN BE WORN IN HOLIDAY FESTIVALS

ALICE FIRST AND LAST WIFE OF THOS. PHILLIP TALKED TO DEATH BY FRIENDS

EPITAPH in Pritchett Cemetery near Boulder, Ill.

A NATURAL TEMPLE COMPRISING WHITE CORAL LIMESTONE COLUMNS AND A GRANITE ROOF CARVED BY THE WATERS OF THE WEB RIVER, IN ETHIOPIA

CAPTAIN JOHN DOUGHTY (1754-1826) FOR THE PERIOD FROM JUNE 20 TO AUG. 12, 1784 COMMANDED THE ENTIRE U.S. ARMY THE U.S. ARMY AT THAT TIME NUMBERED 80 MEN

THE WOLF FISH WHICH GROWS TO A LENGTH OF 6 FEET CAN EASILY CRACK THE SHELL OF A HUGE LOBSTER OR CRAB

THE TOWER A DREAM DESIGNED THE SEA GUARD TOWER in Canton, China, 80 FEET HIGH AND COMPRISING 5 FLOORS, WAS BUILT IN 1388 IN ONE YEAR BY 2 MEN WORKING UNAIDED —THEY BOTH HAD A VISION THAT PERFORMING THE FEAT WOULD ASSURE THEM ETERNAL PEACE

The **RUINS** of the Church of Giessen, Germany, BOMBED IN DECEMBER, 1944, WERE THE SITE OF REGULAR SERVICES FOR A PERIOD OF *5 YEARS*

The **VIPER FISH** of Galapagos *CAN ROTATE ITS EYES IN THEIR SOCKETS*

The **FIRST DOCTOR** A MEDICINE MAN DEPICTED IN A DRAWING ON THE WALLS OF THE Trois Frères Cave, in Southern France, *17,000 YEARS AGO* — THE CAVE MEDICINE MAN IS WEARING A STAG MASK, THE PAWS OF A BEAR, AND THE TAIL OF A WILD HORSE

The **CATHEDRAL** of ST. MAGNUS in Kirkebø on the Faeroe Islands, ON WHICH WORK WAS SUSPENDED IN THE 13th CENTURY FOR LACK OF FUNDS *IS STILL NOT COMPLETED 700 YEARS LATER*

THE STRANGEST POLITICAL CUSTOM IN ALL THE WORLD

The MAYOR of Grammont, Belgium, AND EVERY MEMBER OF HIS TOWN COUNCIL ONCE EACH YEAR FOR THE LAST 672 YEARS *HAVE BEEN REQUIRED TO DRAIN A CUP OF WINE CONTAINING LIVE GOLDFISH*

The RIVER THAT RUNS BACKWARDS
THE SEINE RIVER, near Caudebec, France, DEVELOPS A WAVE 40 FEET HIGH 4 TIMES EACH YEAR —IN MARCH, APRIL, SEPTEMBER AND OCTOBER— *OVERFLOWS ITS BANKS AND REVERSES ITS COURSE FOR 40 MILES, THEN SUDDENLY RETURNS TO NORMAL*

SLOVAKIAN BEEHIVES ARE CARVED TO LOOK LIKE THE BEEKEEPER AND HIS WIFE —SO THE BEES WILL "RECOGNIZE" THEIR OWNERS

BARREL SHRIMP MAKES ITS HOME INSIDE THE HOLLOWED-OUT SKIN OF A SEASQUIRT

YATUNG a village in Tibet WAS CHOSEN AS THE SITE OF A BRITISH TRADE AGENCY IN 1893 BUT ITS LOCATION HIGH IN THE HIMALAYAS MADE IT SO COLD THAT THE BRITISH GAVE THE NAME OF YATUNG TO A VILLAGE IN THE VALLEY *SO THEY COULD TRADE IN GREATER COMFORT*

GIRLS ON THE ISLAND OF CRETE 3,500 YEARS AGO PRACTICED THE DANGEROUS SPORT OF BULL JUMPING—GRABBING A CHARGING BULL BY THE HORNS AND ALLOWING THE ENRAGED ANIMAL TO TOSS THEM ONTO ITS BACK!

THE PLATANNA
a frog of South Africa
CAN JUMP BOTH FORWARD
AND BACKWARD ON
LAND OR IN THE WATER

Potato
CONTAINING
3 OTHER
POTATOES
Grown by
Catherine
Brinkmann,
Idaho Falls,
Idaho

The PROPHET

BISHOP JEAN de BEAUVAIS
(1731-1790) of France
IN A SERMON DELIVERED IN THE
PRESENCE OF KING LOUIS XV ON MARCH
31, 1774, ASSAILED THE MONARCH AND
QUOTED JONAH 3,4: "Yet 40 days
and Nineveh shall be overthrown"
*EXACTLY 40 DAYS LATER
KING LOUIS XV WAS DEAD*

ROAD MARKERS in the Sahara Desert
COMPRISE PILES OF WAFER-THIN STONES
SO CHOSEN TO RESIST THE CONSTANT SANDSTORMS

EPITAPH ON THE GRAVE OF MRS. JOHN Q. ADAMS in the cemetery of Old South Salem, N.Y.

LET ME GO

INDIAN SENTINELS STILL ARE POSTED ON MOUNTAIN-TOPS IN MEXICO EACH JUNE TO WATCH FOR THE RETURN OF EMPEROR MONTEZUMA II, LAST AZTEC RULER OF MEXICO WHO DIED 448 YEARS AGO

HAY MOWED BY THE Gujars of Kashmir IS PROTECTED AGAINST RUIN FROM TORRENTIAL RAINS BY BEING HUNG IN BULKY BRAIDS FROM THE LIMBS OF TREES

ABEL SMITH
A BANKER OF Nottingham, England, AND HIS 5 SONS REPRESENTED DIFFERENT CONSTITUENCIES IN PARLIAMENT *SIMULTANEOUSLY*

A WATER BEETLE CAN KILL A FROG 20 TIMES ITS OWN SIZE

THE **HUNTERS WHO CAPTURE BIRDS WITH THEIR HANDS** SAHARA HUNTERS SEIZE THE IBIS BY HIDING IN THE HIDE OF A CROCODILE AND *GRABBING THE BIRD BY ONE OF ITS LONG LEGS*

THE TASMANIAN SNOW GUM TREE of the Australian Alps IS THE DOWN UNDER CHRISTMAS TREE
BLIZZARDS TWIST THE GUM TREES INTO UNUSUAL SHAPES AND NEAR MOUNT STIRLING, IN TASMANIA, 2 ROWS OF SNOW GUMS HAVE BEEN BENT TO FORM A NATURAL ARCH OVER THE HIGHWAY

ROBERT OWEN
(1771-1858) the British reformer WAS A SCHOOLTEACHER IN HIS NATIVE NEWTOWN, WALES, AT THE AGE OF 7.

EVERY DOORWAY in the village of Mogroum, Chad, Africa IS SHAPED LIKE A KEYHOLE -IN THE BELIEF IT WILL KEEP OUT UNWANTED VISITORS

EEL THAT LIVED WITHOUT EATING FOR 4 YEARS
IT HAD LOST ITS UPPER JAW IN AN ACCIDENT
Zoological Station, Rovigno, Italy

THE GREAT ASTRONOMICAL CLOCK in Münster, Germany, WAS SO MAGNIFICENT THAT ITS MAKER WAS BLINDED TO PREVENT HIM FROM DUPLICATING IT

BUT JUST BEFORE HE WAS MADE SIGHTLESS HE DAMAGED THE CLOCK SO SERIOUSLY IT COULD NOT BE REPAIRED FOR 200 YEARS

ROMAN CENTURIONS ALWAYS CARRIED AS THEIR EMBLEM OF AUTHORITY *A VINE ROD* — ROMAN ARMY REGULATIONS SPECIFIED THAT A SOLDIER COULD BE PUNISHED ONLY BY A FLOGGING ADMINISTERED WITH A ROD MADE OF VINE WOOD

THE MAN WHOSE VOTE CHANGED HISTORY SENATOR EDMUND G. ROSS (1826-1907) of Kansas, AT THE IMPEACHMENT TRIAL OF PRESIDENT ANDREW JOHNSON *CAST THE DECISIVE VOTE THAT ENABLED JOHNSON TO SERVE OUT HIS TERM* HIS ACTION RUINED ROSS POLITICALLY, FINANCIALLY AND SOCIALLY

THE HALL OF THE STONE FLOWERS IN THE CAVE OF TANTALUS, in Salzburg, Austria, ABOUNDS WITH CRYSTAL STALACTITES THAT LOOK LIKE FLOWERS GROWING FROM THE WALLS

STEPHAN GERLACH (1546-1612) DEAN OF THE University of Tübingen, Germany, COULD REMEMBER ALMOST EVERY LINE HE EVER READ —YET HE CONSTANTLY FORGOT HIS OWN NAME

"TIM" A COWHORSE OWNED BY J.D. Wilton of Australia, COULD BALANCE ON A SMALL WOODEN BLOCK

The **PAUJI** A WILD TURKEY of the High Orinoco region of Venezuela HAS A CRY THAT SOUNDS LIKE THE WHISTLE OF A PASSING BULLET

The **GARDEN THAT GROWS IN THE DARK** A SUBTERRANEAN CAVE ON THE GREEK ISLAND OF ANTIPAROS CONTAINS STALAGMITES AND STALACTITES SHAPED LIKE SHRUBS AND FLOWERS

PRINCESS RADZIWILL of Poland AT A MEETING OF THE SKATING CLUB IN ROME, ITALY, IN 1910, DROVE A ROMAN CHARIOT DRAWN BY A LEOPARD AND A LION

BOOM BOOM
A FISH OF British Guiana IS 6 FEET LONG, HAS A MOUTH A FOOT WIDE AND *MAKES A NOISE LIKE THE BOOMING OF A DRUM*

JOHANN KUNCKEL
(1630-1703) an alchemist LABORED IN VAIN HIS ENTIRE LIFETIME TO CONVERT BASE METAL INTO GOLD, BUT DISCOVERED DURING HIS EXPERIMENTS: *SULPHIDE OF TIN, ARTIFICIAL SULPHUR, NITRIC ETHER, AND THE WAY TO MAKE RUBY GLASS*

TRIBAL CHIEFS
of the Fiji Islands STAND WHILE THEIR INFERIORS REST CROSSLEGGED ON THE GROUND *THE FIJIAN WORD FOR CHIEF IS "TU"- MEANING "TO STAND"*

THE CROOKED HOUSE in Vitte, Germany, WAS BUILT TO LOOK AS IF IT WERE IN IMMINENT DANGER OF COLLAPSE *TO KEEP OUT WITCHES*

FARMERS in New Guinea *ARE ALWAYS WOMEN* THE MEN JUST STAND GUARD WHILE THE WOMEN WORK

A MECHANICAL STATUE DEPICTING 2 WORSHIPERS POURING A LIBATION FOR THE GODS WAS EXHIBITED THROUGHOUT ANCIENT EGYPT 1,900 YEARS AGO

THE MEAT OF THE GREENLAND WHALE IS HIGHLY POISONOUS IF EATEN FRESH —YET WHOLESOME IF AGED UNTIL IT IS ALMOST PUTRID

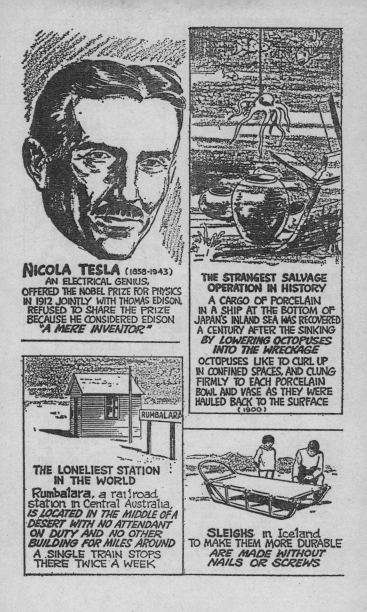

NICOLA TESLA (1858-1943)

AN ELECTRICAL GENIUS, OFFERED THE NOBEL PRIZE FOR PHYSICS IN 1912 JOINTLY WITH THOMAS EDISON, REFUSED TO SHARE THE PRIZE BECAUSE HE CONSIDERED EDISON *"A MERE INVENTOR"*

THE STRANGEST SALVAGE OPERATION IN HISTORY

A CARGO OF PORCELAIN IN A SHIP AT THE BOTTOM OF JAPAN'S INLAND SEA WAS RECOVERED A CENTURY AFTER THE SINKING *BY LOWERING OCTOPUSES INTO THE WRECKAGE* OCTOPUSES LIKE TO CURL UP IN CONFINED SPACES, AND CLUNG FIRMLY TO EACH PORCELAIN BOWL AND VASE AS THEY WERE HAULED BACK TO THE SURFACE (1900)

THE LONELIEST STATION IN THE WORLD

Rumbalara, a railroad station in Central Australia, *IS LOCATED IN THE MIDDLE OF A DESERT WITH NO ATTENDANT ON DUTY AND NO OTHER BUILDING FOR MILES AROUND* A SINGLE TRAIN STOPS THERE TWICE A WEEK

SLEIGHS in Iceland

TO MAKE THEM MORE DURABLE *ARE MADE WITHOUT NAILS OR SCREWS*

A **LOBSTER** SHEDS ITS TAIL 20 TIMES

A **STALK** of **MEXICAN CORN** grown from seeds by Simon C. Noyes, of Landaff, N.H., WAS CUT DOWN BEFORE IT HAD ACHIEVED FULL GROWTH —YET IN 4 MONTHS IT REACHED A HEIGHT OF 11 FEET. A CIRCUMFERENCE OF 8½ INCHES, AND HAD LEAVES 45 INCHES LONG.

DR. EMIL ZSIGMONDY (1861-1885) famed Austrian mountain climber SCALED 100 PEAKS THAT WERE MORE THAN 10,000 FEET HIGH AND HAD 14 NEAR-FATAL FALLS HE DIED IN HIS 15th FALL AT THE AGE OF 24.

TEENAGERS
in the Sudan, Africa,
MUST WEAR A HEADDRESS FROM
WHICH 3 SHELLS DANGLE IN
FRONT OF THEIR FACE
THEY HAVE TO WALK IN A
DIGNIFIED MANNER OR
THE SHELLS WILL BOUNCE
AGAINST THEIR NOSE

**THE STRANGEST PLACE OF
REVERENCE IN THE WORLD**
AN EMPTY GRAVE
MARKING THE SPOT WHERE
A ROBBER ATTEMPTED TO
ASSASSINATE JOSE ANTONIO PAEZ
REVOLUTIONARY HERO OF VENEZUELA
IS REVERED AND GUARDED
BY LOCAL PEASANTS
THE BANDIT'S BODY ACTUALLY
WAS NEVER BURIED THERE
BUT PEASANTS ADD STONES
TO ITS COVER BECAUSE THEY
FEEL THAT ANYONE HAVING
HAD CONTACT WITH THEIR HERO
IS WORTHY OF REVERENCE
EVEN AN ATTEMPTED ASSASSIN

A PUBLIC DRINKING
FOUNTAIN in Burgos, Spain,
GUSHES FORTH WATER AT
A TEMPERATURE OF
150 DEGREES FAHRENHEIT

AN
ELEPHANT
in the
Franconi
Circus
EXPERTLY
PLAYED THE
HARMONICA
1820

THE DREAM THAT BECAME REALITY

ROSE HILL COLLEGE IN THE BRONX, N.Y., WHICH LATER BECAME FORDHAM UNIVERSITY APPEARED TO WILLIAM HENNEN, OF BAVARIA, IN A DREAM SO VIVIDLY THAT HE TRAVELED *THROUGH GERMANY, HOLLAND, FRANCE AND THE U.S. IN SEARCH OF IT* HE FOUND IT IN 1846-34 YEARS AFTER HIS DREAM-AND BECAME A MEMBER OF ITS FACULTY

GENERAL JAN CHRISTIAN SMUTS
(1870-1950) commander-in-chief of the Boers
CARRIED A RIFLE THROUGHOUT THE BOER WAR
YET NEVER FIRED A SINGLE SHOT

COW WITH A HEART ON ITS FOREHEAD
Owned by John W. Rightmer San Antonio, Texas

UNE PERSONNE IN FRENCH *MEANS "A PERSON"*- BUT PERSONNE WITHOUT THE ARTICLE MEANS "NOBODY"

KING CHARLES XII
of Sweden
WHO WAS DEFEATED BY CZAR PETER THE GREAT OF RUSSIA IN THE BATTLE OF POLTAVA, WAS SO ILL AT THE TIME THAT HE WAS CARRIED ONTO THE BATTLEFIELD ON A STRETCHER-WITH A SPECIAL GUARD OF 24 SOLDIERS

A DIRECT HIT BY THE RUSSIAN ARTILLERY SMASHED THE STRETCHER AND KILLED 21 OF HIS GUARD-BUT THE MONARCH ESCAPED WITHOUT A SCRATCH (July 8, 1709)

WOMEN
of the Pardhan Tribe of India
ARE PUNISHED FOR TARDINESS OR LAZINESS *BY BEING YOKED TO A PLOW- BESIDE A BULLOCK*

PEARL DUCK
A SPECIALTY OF THE THREE PROVENÇAL 'BROTHERS' RESTAURANT IN PARIS, FRANCE, IN 1791, WAS ALWAYS GARNISHED *WITH A $1,000 STRING OF ORIENTAL PEARLS—* THE DINER HAD TO RETURN THE PEARLS

HATS DESIGNED TO BE UNFLATTERING
WOMEN of Banjermasin, Borneo, FOR 100 YEARS HAVE WORN HUGE HATS *WHICH HIDE THEIR BEAUTY—* THE CUSTOM STARTED WHEN THE SULTAN OF BORNEO WOULD SEIZE ANY WOMAN WHOSE FACE APPEALED TO HIM

THE **SABLE ANTELOPE** of Africa *IS A MATCH FOR A LION*

KITCHEN FLOORS in rural areas of the District of Engadine, Switzerland, ARE STILL PAVED WITH COBBLESTONES—*IN THE BELIEF THAT WALKING ON THEM BAREFOOTED WILL STRENGTHEN THE FEET*

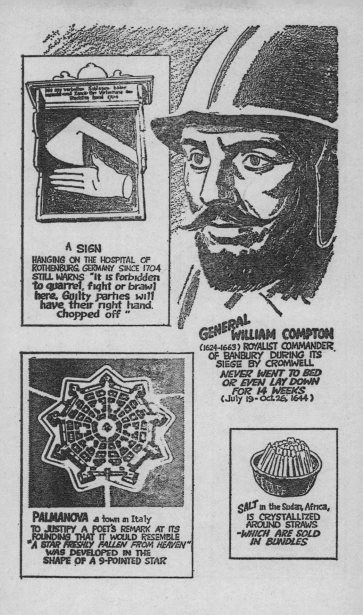

A SIGN
HANGING ON THE HOSPITAL OF
ROTHENBURG, GERMANY SINCE 1704
STILL WARNS "It is forbidden
to quarrel, fight or brawl
here. Guilty parties will
have their right hand
chopped off "

GENERAL WILLIAM COMPTON
(1624-1663) ROYALIST COMMANDER
OF BANBURY DURING ITS
SIEGE BY CROMWELL
*NEVER WENT TO BED
OR EVEN LAY DOWN
FOR 14 WEEKS*
(July 19 - Oct. 26, 1644)

PALMANOVA a town in Italy
TO JUSTIFY A POET'S REMARK AT ITS
FOUNDING THAT IT WOULD RESEMBLE
"A STAR *FRESHLY FALLEN FROM HEAVEN*"
WAS DEVELOPED IN THE
SHAPE OF A 9-POINTED STAR

SALT in the Sudan, Africa,
IS CRYSTALLIZED
AROUND STRAWS
-WHICH ARE SOLD
IN BUNDLES

THE FIRST THANKSGIVING
Berkeley Hundred
A TOBACCO PLANTATION LOCATED
near Jamestown Island, Va.,
WAS THE SCENE OF THE FIRST
THANKSGIVING FEAST IN AMERICA
ON *DECEMBER 3, 1619*
38 MEN LANDED HERE AND HELD
A THANKSGIVING DAY CELEBRATION
ALMOST A YEAR BEFORE
THE PILGRIMS LANDED AT
PLYMOUTH ROCK

"FRANKLIN
WIRES"
ADORNED THE
HATS OF CHIC
PARISIAN WOMEN
IN 1776
IN HONOR OF
BENJAMIN
FRANKLIN'S
INVENTION – *THE
LIGHTNING ROD*

THE WINDMILL OF
PIERRE EMILE BOUDEVILLE,
THE LAST MILLER OF
VERZENAY, FRANCE, WAS
STOPPED WHEN HE DIED IN 1903
–AND AS A MEMORIAL TO HIM
HAS NOT BEEN PERMITTED
TO TURN FOR 64 YEARS

BEARS
TURN ON THE
SPRINKLING
SYSTEM
AT THE
JASPER PARK
GOLF COURSE
ON WARM DAYS
Canadian
Rockies

MILTON DOUGLAS of Murfreesboro, Tennessee, ON A VISIT TO ST. AUGUSTINE, FLORIDA, FOUND A STREET MARKER BEARING HIS FULL NAME AT *MILTON* STREET AND *DOUGLAS* AVENUE

THE STEEPLE of the CHURCH of ST. PETER, in Riga, Latvia, *LEANS 2 FEET OFF CENTER*

JOOST VAN CLEVE (1479-1529) of Antwerp ONE OF THE MOST CELEBRATED PAINTERS OF HIS TIME *ALWAYS PAINTED PICTURES ON BOTH SIDES OF THE CANVAS*

THE "H" TREE
Near Doboj, Yugoslavia

Submitted by Danilo Alargic
Belgrade, Yugoslavia

THE MAN WHO WAS IN LOVE WITH HIS SHADOW
WILLIE BEYER
a businessman of Halberstadt, Germany,
TO VIEW THE BROCKEN SPECTER, AN
ENORMOUSLY MAGNIFIED SHADOW CAST
UPON THE CLOUDS FROM MOUNT BROCKEN
WHEN THE SUN IS LOW
*CLIMBED 3,733 FEET TO THE TOP
OF THE MOUNTAIN·650 TIMES*

A **BAYONET**
USED BY THE
ARMY IN
1874 WAS
DESIGNED
SO IT ALSO
SERVED AS
A SHOVEL

THE 6-HORSE SLEIGH used by the mother of Czar Peter the Great, of Russia,
WAS ALWAYS ACCOMPANIED BY 12 GROOMS-ONE FOR EACH HORSE-
AND 6 OTHERS WHO PUSHED THE SLEIGH TO INCREASE ITS
SPEED -ALL THE GROOMS HAD TO RUN STEADILY FOR MILES

THE MOST COURAGEOUS PATIENT IN ALL HISTORY

GIOVANNI dei MEDICI (1498-1526) an Italian military leader WHEN TOLD THAT HIS LEG WOULD BE AMPUTATED, WAVED AWAY THE 10 MEN ASSIGNED TO HOLD HIM DOWN -AND HELD THE TORCH THAT ILLUMINATED HIS OWN OPERATION

THE AMMAIKIN TEMPLE in Bangkok, Thailand, WAS CONSTRUCTED TO SHELTER A SINGLE FOOTPRINT OF BUDDHA

DOMENICO AULISIO

(1639-1717) of Naples, Italy, AT THE AGE OF 19 TAUGHT POETRY AT THE UNIVERSITY OF NAPLES AND SIMULTANEOUSLY LECTURED ON MILITARY FORTIFICATIONS AT THE ITALIAN MILITARY ACADEMY

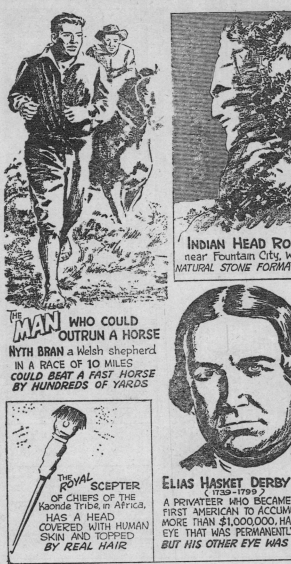

INDIAN HEAD ROCK
near Fountain City, Wis.,
NATURAL STONE FORMATION

THE **MAN** WHO COULD
OUTRUN A HORSE

NYTH BRAN a Welsh shepherd
IN A RACE OF 10 MILES
*COULD BEAT A FAST HORSE
BY HUNDREDS OF YARDS*

THE ROYAL SCEPTER
OF CHIEFS OF THE
Kaonde Tribe, in Africa,
HAS A HEAD
COVERED WITH HUMAN
SKIN AND TOPPED
BY REAL HAIR

ELIAS HASKET DERBY
(1739-1799)
A PRIVATEER WHO BECAME THE
FIRST AMERICAN TO ACCUMULATE
MORE THAN $1,000,000, HAD ONE
EYE THAT WAS PERMANENTLY BLACK
BUT HIS OTHER EYE WAS BLUE

2 ELEPHANTS
ARE PORTRAYED IN A MAYA SCULPTURE ON THE TEMPLE OF COPAN, HONDURAS —YET THE SCULPTURE PRE-DATES COLUMBUS' VOYAGES, AND ELEPHANTS WERE UNKNOWN IN THE NEW WORLD

THE **SPANISH** TWIST
2 OLIVE TREES in the Enchanted forest of Mallorca, Spain, HAVE BEEN ENTWINED FOR 1,000 YEARS

CAPTAIN THOMAS P. LEATHERS
(1816-1889) a native of Kentucky, WAS SO FOND OF HIS ADOPTED TOWN OF NATCHEZ, MISS., THAT *HE NAMED 7 SUCCESSIVE STEAMBOATS "THE NATCHEZ"* HE WAS A HUGE MAN AND HAD MANY NARROW ESCAPES FROM DEATH, BUT HE WAS FINALLY KILLED IN NEW ORLEANS AT 73 *BY A HIT-AND-RUN BICYCLE*

"BILLIE" A HORSE THAT PULLED SHIPS ALONG THE RHINE RIVER between Mainz and Frankfurt, Germany, LABORED AT THAT TASK CONTINUOUSLY FOR 39 YEARS

THE BELL OF THE S.S. AMERICA, LAST OF THE MISSISSIPPI RIVER COTTON PACKETS, HAS BEEN ERECTED AS A MEMORIAL OVER THE GRAVES OF THE BOAT'S OWNERS, CAPTAIN AND MRS. LEVERRIER COOLEY Metairie Cemetery, New Orleans, La.

PHILIPPE de VENDOME (1655-1727) ONE OF THE WEALTHIEST ARISTOCRATS OF FRANCE, DRANK SO HEAVILY THAT HE HAD TO BE CARRIED TO HIS BED EVERY NIGHT FOR 30 YEARS

FRANCESCO CONTARINI (1556-1624)
WHO WAS BORN ON SEPT. 8th
WAS APPOINTED TO 24 DIFFERENT
POSTS IN THE VENETIAN REPUBLIC
EACH TIME ON SEPTEMBER 8th
WE WAS ELECTED DOGE OF VENICE,
HIGHEST OFFICE IN THE LAND,
ALSO ON SEPTEMBER 8th

THE **SAHARA "SNAKE PIT"**
NATIVES OF FEZZAN
in the Sahara desert
BELIEVE THEY CAN CURE
MENTALLY DISTURBED RELATIVES
*BY LEAVING THEM FOR 7
DAYS IN THIS DEEP WELL*

JACK JONES son of Mr. and Mrs.
James Jones
of Rockford, Ill.
COULD SIT UP UNASSISTED
ONE WEEK AFTER HIS BIRTH

THE GREAT LIGHTHOUSE
IN THE HARBOR OF
Swinoujscie, Poland,
IS ALSO A WORKING WINDMILL

AN **IDOL** OF FORBIDDING MIEN at Katmandu, Nepal, MARKS EACH FESTIVE DAY BY SPOUTING A STEADY *STREAM OF CHAMPAGNE*

A **FARM GIRL** in Coruña, Spain, OFTEN WALKS 20 MILES TO MARKET *BALANCING 22 CHICKENS ON HER HEAD*

SHADOWS FOR THE WALLS OF DEATH

ROBERT C.KEDZIE

100 BOOKS ENTITLED "SHADOWS FOR THE WALLS OF DEATH" WERE PREPARED BY DR. ROBERT C. KEDZIE, A CHEMISTRY PROFESSOR, FROM ROLLS OF WALLPAPER AND SENT TO LEADING LIBRARIES IN 1902, -TO DRAMATIZE THE DANGER IN THE USE OF ARSENIC TO TINT WALLPAPER- THE PRACTICE WAS DISCONTINUED

THE **WALLS**
OF THE LIBRARY IN THE ROYAL
RESIDENCE OF MARLBOROUGH
HOUSE, IN LONDON, ARE
LINED WITH LEATHER SPINES
OF *NON-EXISTING BOOKS,*
BEARING IMAGINARY TITLES

The **FOREST**
FOUNTAINS
of SUMATRA
A NATIVE TRAVELING
THROUGH THE TROPICAL
FORESTS CAN CHOP OFF A
SECTION OF A LIANA PLANT
—AND DRINK HIS FILL OF
SWEET WATER

YOUNG
WOOD
SWALLOWS
A SPECIES
OF BIRDS IN
NEW GUINEA
DO NOT LEAVE
THE NEST WHEN
THEY GROW UP—
THEY STAY AND
HELP THEIR PARENTS
FEED THE NEXT BROOD

THE PERFECT PAIR
FRANCIS AND MARY HUNTRODDS
of Whitby, England,
WERE BOTH BORN ON THE SAME DAY,
SEPTEMBER 19, 1600, WERE MARRIED ON
THEIR BIRTHDAY — *AND BOTH DIED
IN 1680 ON THEIR BIRTHDAY*

A MEMORIAL
ERECTED IN LOGAN CANYON, UTAH,
TO "OLD EPHRAIM," A GRIZZLY BEAR,
*ALTHOUGH FOR YEARS HE
HAD KILLED SHEEP AND CATTLE
AS WELL AS WILD GAME*

"OLD EPHRAIM'S" MEMORIAL
IS 9'11½" HIGH, WHICH WAS
HOW HIGH THE GRIZZLY
TOWERED ON HIS HIND FEET,
AND IT WEIGHS THE SAME
AS THE BEAR
—1,100 POUNDS

Tronc de l'heureuse
délivrance

A COLLECTION BOX
IN THE PRISON
at Thumai, Belgium,
FOR 200 YEARS
HAS BEEN MARKED
"For a happy delivery"
THE PHRASE IS CONSIDERED
EQUALLY APT FOR WOMEN
CONTRIBUTORS—AND THE
PRISONERS WHO ARE
THE BENEFICIARIES

THE CUIRASS FISH
of British
Guiana
OFTEN SPENDS
THE NIGHT ON
DRY LAND

THE **STONE HOUSES** of the Ighchen Tribe of Algeria ARE BUILT WITH LOOSELY PILED STONES BECAUSE A CHIEFTAIN BECAME MORTALLY ILL ON A VISIT TO PARIS, FRANCE, IN 1880 AND BLAMED HIS SICKNESS ON THE MORTAR IN HIS HOTEL'S WALLS

EMPRESS ELIZABETH I
(1709-1762) of Russia
HAD A WARDROBE OF 15,000 DRESSES— ALL PINK

A **BABY** BORN TO THE Amharas of Ethiopia IS GIVEN AS A NAME *THE FIRST WORD UTTERED BY THE MOTHER AFTER THE INFANT'S BIRTH*

MOUNT MAI CHI SHAN
China
HAS 196 TEMPLES CARVED IN ITS SOLID ROCK FOR 1,000 YEARS PILGRIMS HAVE BEEN ABLE TO REACH THEM ONLY BY CLIMBING RICKETY LADDERS AND SCAFFOLDING

THE **MOUNT SUNG PAGODA**
China
BUILT 1,400 YEARS AGO IS THE ONLY PAGODA IN THE COUNTRY WITH 12 SIDES

THE BEE FLY
DEPOSITS ITS EGGS IN THE NEST OF A DIGGER WASP SO THAT THE BEE FLY'S LARVA *CAN SHARE THE WASP'S FOOD SUPPLY*

A HERMIT'S CAVE in Kediri, Java, ITS ENTRANCE CARVED TO RESEMBLE A MONSTER WITH A WIDE-OPEN MOUTH

Dr. WILLIAM GILBERT
(1544-1603) of Colchester, England,
PHYSICIAN TO QUEEN ELIZABETH, WAS THE FIRST TO WRITE ABOUT ELECTRICITY

THE EUROPEAN TENCH
A FISH COMMONLY SOLD IN THE MARKETS CAN LIVE OUT OF WATER FOR 24 HOURS IN ANCIENT TIMES, BECAUSE OF ITS HARDINESS, IT WAS BELIEVED THAT MERELY TOUCHING A TENCH COULD MAKE A SICK MAN WELL

THE SKYTALE USED IN ancient Sparta FOR SECRET MESSAGES

A STRIP OF PARCHMENT WAS WRAPPED SPIRALLY AROUND A STICK AND THE MESSAGE WRITTEN ON ITS FOLDS COULD LATER BE READ ONLY WHEN IT WAS WOUND IN THE SAME WAY ON AN IDENTICAL STICK

FREIGHT TRAINS
of the Oahu Railway of Hawaii
DURING THE 72 YEARS FROM
1889 TO 1961 HAD NO CABOOSES
*AND THE CREWS HAD TO
RIDE ATOP THE BOXCARS*

KING BELA II of Hungary
WAS ELECTED MONARCH AND RULED
THE COUNTRY FOR 10 YEARS (1131-1141)
-ALTHOUGH HE WAS TOTALLY BLIND
HIS UNCLE, KING KOLOMAN, HAD
BLINDED BELA IN THE BELIEF IT
WOULD MAKE HIM INCAPABLE OF
SUCCEEDING TO THE THRONE

THE "OSTRICH" FROG-
THE WESTERN FROG
AT THE FIRST SIGN
OF DANGER
*BURIES ITS HEAD
IN THE MUD*

THE **LAKE** OF POISON, near Naliabganj, India – FOR CENTURIES CRIMINALS
WERE EXECUTED BY BEING FORCED TO DRINK ITS WATER

KING HUGH CAPET of France
(938-996)
FOUNDER OF THE CAPETIAN DYNASTY
WAS GIVEN THE NAME CAPET—
MEANING CAP—BECAUSE AS AN
EXUBERANT PRINCE HE OFTEN
KNOCKED THE CAPS OFF PASSERSBY

A **GREAT TREE**
OVERLOOKING THE WATERFALLS
OF THE TSHOPO RIVER, AT
STANLEYVILLE, IN THE CONGO,
IS SHAPED BY NATURE
*IN THE FORM OF
A HUGE CROSS*

ANDERS LJUNG of
Ljungby, Sweden,
WHO MARRIED
TWICE,
HAD 7 DAUGHTERS
BY HIS FIRST
WIFE AND
7 SONS
BY HIS
SECOND

TREES GROW FROM THE STONE STAIRWAY OF THE GREAT TEMPLE OF COPAN, IN HONDURAS —THE RESULT OF SEEDS DROPPED BY WORSHIPERS TO FEED THE SANCTUARY'S BIRDS

LEONARD COLE
(1788-1857) SCHOOLMASTER of West Union, Ohio
WHEN ANY BOY MISBEHAVED ALWAYS WHIPPED EVERY YOUNGSTER IN THE SCHOOL

ÉMILE ANTHOINE
President of the French Walking Union,
WON 800 PROFESSIONAL WALKING CONTESTS
—COVERING A TOTAL OF 600,000 MILES

THE **CREDENTIAL** OF PAPAL AMBASSADORS IN the 15th Century
WAS A HUGE SILVER RING TOO LARGE TO WEAR
WHICH WAS CARRIED ON STATE OCCASIONS ON A TRAY

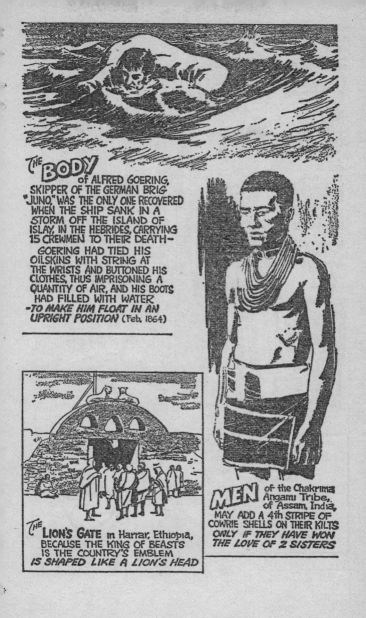

THE BODY of ALFRED GOERING, SKIPPER OF THE GERMAN BRIG "JUNO," WAS THE ONLY ONE RECOVERED WHEN THE SHIP SANK IN A STORM OFF THE ISLAND OF ISLAY, IN THE HEBRIDES, CARRYING 15 CREWMEN TO THEIR DEATH—

GOERING HAD TIED HIS OILSKINS WITH STRING AT THE WRISTS AND BUTTONED HIS CLOTHES, THUS IMPRISONING A QUANTITY OF AIR, AND HIS BOOTS HAD FILLED WITH WATER —TO MAKE HIM FLOAT IN AN UPRIGHT POSITION (Feb. 1864)

THE LION'S GATE in Harrar, Ethiopia, BECAUSE THE KING OF BEASTS IS THE COUNTRY'S EMBLEM IS SHAPED LIKE A LION'S HEAD

MEN of the Chakrima Angami Tribe, of Assam, India, MAY ADD A 4th STRIPE OF COWRIE SHELLS ON THEIR KILTS ONLY IF THEY HAVE WON THE LOVE OF 2 SISTERS

THE **SAMSON WALTZ**

THE **BUTCHERS** of Tamsweg, Austria, ANNUALLY FOR THE LAST 200 YEARS HAVE DANCED IN A COLORFUL FESTIVAL WEARING A FRAMEWORK MAKING THEM RESEMBLE THE BIBLICAL GIANT —AND 18 FEET TALL

THE **GATEWAY TO SHAME**
THE CHURCH OF NÖRDLINGEN in Germany IN THE 16th CENTURY WAS CONVERTED INTO A BARN AND YEARS LATER ITS ENTRANCE WAS CARVED ELABORATELY WITH *LIKENESSES OF THE WORKERS WHO HAD PERFORMED THE DESECRATION*

JUSTICE **BERNARD SHAW** of Cyprus WAS SHOT THROUGH THE THROAT, NECK AND EAR—YET HE WAS PRESIDING AGAIN AS A TRIAL JUDGE ONLY 10 DAYS LATER 1957

THE **GREAT ABYSSINIAN HORNBILL** *WHEN IT IS TIRED USES ITS LONG BILL AS A CANE*

VIRGINIE **GHESQUIÈRE** of Deulement, France, DISGUISED AS A BOY *FOUGHT IN THE FRENCH ARMY FOR 6 YEARS AND WAS PROMOTED TO SERGEANT* HER SECRET WAS DISCOVERED IN 1812 ONLY BECAUSE SHE WAS WOUNDED IN BATTLE

PEKING the Chinese capital WHEN INVADED FOR THE FIRST TIME IN HISTORY BY A EUROPEAN ARMY WAS DEFENDED ONLY BY A FEW CHINESE WHO ATTEMPTED TO FRIGHTEN OFF THE ENEMY BY WAVING *PAPER TIGERS AND DRAGONS* (1860)

THE **SHELL** of the **LITTLE POSTHORN** a deep-sea squid *IS INSIDE ITS BODY* THE SHELL IS FILLED WITH A GAS THAT HELPS THE SQUID MAINTAIN ITS EQUILIBRIUM IN THE WATER

THE **SIGNATURE** OF **CHARLEMAGNE** First holy Roman Emperor and king of the Franks WAS MERELY A MARK WHICH HE MADE IN THE CENTER OF HIS MONOGRAM—AFTER IT HAD BEEN *WRITTEN BY A SCRIBE* *CHARLEMAGNE NEVER LEARNED TO SIGN HIS NAME*

THE ANSON NORTHRUP
a Minnesota River boat
WAS DISASSEMBLED IN 1859,
TRANSPORTED OVERLAND
TO MOORHEAD, MINN., AND
*SERVED FOR YEARS ON THE
RED RIVER OF THE NORTH*

"THISBEE" A
MALTESE DOG
THAT WAS THE
PET OF MARIE
ANTOINETTE
*JUMPED TO ITS
DEATH FROM
THE ST. MICHEL
BRIDGE OVER
THE SEINE ON
THE DAY THE
QUEEN DIED ON
THE GUILLOTINE*
Oct. 16, 1793

MILO
of Crotona
THE MOST FAMOUS GREEK WRESTLER
OF ANCIENT TIMES, WOULD CURL HIS
FINGERS AROUND A POMEGRANATE
*—AND NO MAN EVER PRIED OPEN
HIS GRIP OR DAMAGED THE FRUIT*

THE PADDLE FISH
(Polyodon reticulatus) of the MISSISSIPPI
HAS A SNOUT AS LONG AS ITS BODY

GODOLPHIN HOUSE
in Helston, England,
AND ITS ENTIRE ESTATE WERE
LOST TO THE St AUBYNS FAMILY
IN A BET ON A SNAIL RACE

THE WINNER, BECAUSE HE WON
ON A TECHNICALITY, ALLOWED
THE GODOLPHINS TO REMAIN
IN THE HOUSE AND FOR YEARS
COLLECTED AN ANNUAL RENT
OF 66 CENTS

WEALTHY PILGRIMS
SEEKING THE SPIRITUAL
BENEFITS OF A 20,000-FOOT
CLIMB TO TEMPLES ATOP
MOUNTAINS IN NEPAL, OFTEN
MAKE THE TWO-WEEK ASCENT IN
*BASKETS ATOP THE SHOULDERS
OF HUSKY PORTERS*

THE STONE MONK
on Mount Dore, France,
NATURAL ROCK FORMATION

Lena Stumpf
A COLLEGE STUDENT of Leipzig, Germany, PARALYZED IN BOTH LEGS AS THE RESULT OF DIPHTHERIA, SPENT 2½ YEARS IN BED AND WAS TOLD BY DOCTORS THAT HER CASE WAS HOPELESS. *SHE DEVISED A SET OF EXERCISES HERSELF AND WON THE WEST GERMAN PENTATHLON CHAMPIONSHIP (HIGH JUMP, SPEAR THROWING, BROAD JUMP, DISCUS AND RUNNING) IN BOTH OF THE NEXT 2 YEARS*

NICON
(50-150) AN ARCHITECT of Pergamum, Asia Minor, ACCORDING TO HIS SON, GALEN, WHO WAS CONSIDERED THE GREATEST PHYSICIAN OF HIS ERA, LIVED TO THE AGE OF 100 BECAUSE HE NEVER *ATE A PIECE OF FRUIT*

CAMPIONE
a village with a population of 578 IS ON THE SHORE OF LAKE LUGANO, SWITZERLAND, AND IS COMPLETELY SURROUNDED BY SWISS TERRITORY *- YET IT IS PART OF ITALY*

THE **BOAT** CARRYING COAL TO LIGHT THE
NEWLY ERECTED LIGHTHOUSE OF ST. AGNES
ON THE SCILLY ISLES, ENGLAND,
FOR THE FIRST TIME
*- HIT THAT LIGHTHOUSE IN THE DARKNESS
AND WAS WRECKED*
Oct. 30, 1680

THE **LAZY BLOSSOMS**
AS BLOOMS OF THE
DESERT CHRISTMAS
CACTUS ARE CALLED-
*FOLD THEIR PETALS
EVERY NIGHT AND DO
NOT OPEN THEM TILL
3 P.M. THE NEXT DAY*

THE **GREATEST FINGER PAINTER**
KORNELIS KETEL (1548-1602)
PAINTED SOME OF HIS GREATEST
MASTERPIECES WITHOUT THE USE
OF A BRUSH - *USING ONLY
HIS FINGERS OR TOES*

HAYSTACK ROCK near Astoria, Oregon
NATURAL STONE FORMATION

SEA DOG
A BOXER MASCOT OF THE "CHAMOIS," A FRENCH NAVAL VESSEL, LEFT BEHIND AT PORT SAID, EGYPT, WAS WAITING ON THE WHARF WHEN THE SHIP REACHED SAIGON - *6,000 MILES AWAY* -
THE DOG HAD STOWED AWAY ON A FASTER VESSEL HEADED FOR THE SAME PORT AS THE "CHAMOIS" (1940)

THE OBLONG SUNFISH
IS SO RARELY SEEN THAT WHEN IT APPEARS IN HONOLULU BAY HAWAIIANS REVERENTLY RETURN IT TO THE SEA IN THE BELIEF IT IS THE *ANCESTOR GOD OF ALL MACKERELS AND BONITOS*

MARC-ANTOINE OUDINET (1643-1712)
WHO LATER BECAME A FAMED FRENCH COIN EXPERT, MEMORIZED ALL 12 BOOKS OF VIRGIL'S "AENEID" - *10,000 LINES OF POETRY* - IN A SINGLE WEEK AT THE AGE OF 12

CHARLES de VOLVIRE
of Bois de la Roche, France, WAS THE FATHER OF A SAINT, A PRIEST AND 7 NUNS

THE STONE KNIFE USED BY THE CAVEMEN WAS MORE EFFICIENT THAN MODERN CUTLERY IN CUTTING THE BONES OF FRESHLY KILLED ANIMALS

THE MARTYR WHO GAVE HIS LIFE FOR STRANGERS
YUAN CH'ANG CHINESE GOVERNOR OF HANGCHOW DURING THE BOXER REBELLION RECEIVED A TELEGRAM FROM THE CHINESE EMPRESS ORDERING HIM *TO EXTERMINATE ALL FOREIGNERS* — HE SAVED THE LIVES OF THE EUROPEANS BY CHANGING THE WORD "EXTERMINATE" TO "PROTECT" — *BUT WAS HIMSELF SAWED IN TWO AS PUNISHMENT*

THE NUORO CHURCH in Sardinia, Italy; WAS CONSTRUCTED TO LOOK LIKE A PRIMITIVE CHURCH THAT HAD BEEN *CARVED OUT OF SOLID ROCK ON THAT SPOT*

SIMON'S CENTENNIAL BITTERS
A POPULAR REMEDY IN NEW ENGLAND IN 1876 WAS SOLD IN A BOTTLE SHAPED LIKE A BUST *OF GEORGE WASHINGTON*

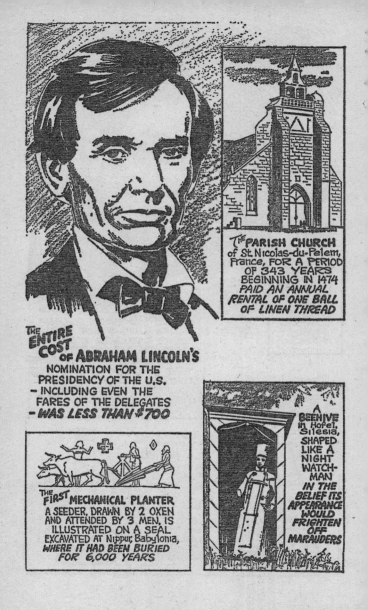

THE PARISH CHURCH of St. Nicolas-du-Pelem, France, FOR A PERIOD OF 343 YEARS BEGINNING IN 1474 PAID AN ANNUAL RENTAL OF ONE BALL OF LINEN THREAD

THE ENTIRE COST of ABRAHAM LINCOLN'S NOMINATION FOR THE PRESIDENCY OF THE U.S. - INCLUDING EVEN THE FARES OF THE DELEGATES - WAS LESS THAN $700

THE FIRST MECHANICAL PLANTER A SEEDER, DRAWN BY 2 OXEN AND ATTENDED BY 3 MEN, IS ILLUSTRATED ON A SEAL EXCAVATED AT Nippur, Babylonia, WHERE IT HAD BEEN BURIED FOR 6,000 YEARS

A BEEHIVE in Hofel, Silesia, SHAPED LIKE A NIGHT WATCH-MAN IN THE BELIEF ITS APPEARANCE WOULD FRIGHTEN OFF MARAUDERS

THE **SANCTUARY OF SIDI el YAMANI** in T'Zenin, Morocco, IS COVERED WITH GOBS OF CLAY BECAUSE PILGRIMS WHISPER THEIR WRONGDOINGS TO THE WALLS THEN PILE WET CLAY OVER THE SPOT *TO MODESTLY HIDE THEIR SINS*

THE **PHOTOGRAPH** OF HER FATHER SNAPPED IN SHAP, ENGLAND, IN 1920 BY ELIZABETH PRIESTLEY, WHO WAS THEN 20 YEARS OF AGE, MYSTERIOUSLY SHOWED IN THE RIGHT BACKGROUND *A LIKENESS OF ELIZABETH HERSELF WHEN SHE WAS 5 YEARS OF AGE*

THE **TOWN OF ELEVA,** Wisconsin, GETS ITS NAME FROM THE FACT THAT YEARS AGO PAINTERS LEFT **UNFINISHED A SIGN IDENTIFYING A GRAIN ELEVATOR** *THEY PAINTED THE LETTERS ELEVA - AND THEN STOPPED WORK UNTIL THE END OF THE WINTER*

THE **SPINES** of **THORNBER'S CHOLLA** a cactus found in Arizona ARE SO PAINFUL TO REMOVE FROM THE HUMAN BODY THAT MANY DOCTORS SUGGEST *THEY BE LEFT TO WORK THEIR OWN WAY OUT THROUGH THE SKIN*

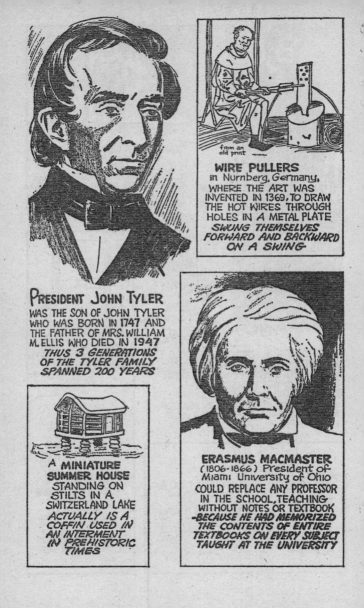

WIRE PULLERS
in Nurnberg, Germany, WHERE THE ART WAS INVENTED IN 1369, TO DRAW THE HOT WIRES THROUGH HOLES IN A METAL PLATE *SWUNG THEMSELVES FORWARD AND BACKWARD ON A SWING·*

from an old print

PRESIDENT JOHN TYLER
WAS THE SON OF JOHN TYLER WHO WAS BORN IN 1747 AND THE FATHER OF MRS. WILLIAM M. ELLIS WHO DIED IN 1947 *THUS 3 GENERATIONS OF THE TYLER FAMILY SPANNED 200 YEARS*

A MINIATURE SUMMER HOUSE STANDING ON STILTS IN A SWITZERLAND LAKE *ACTUALLY IS A COFFIN USED IN AN INTERMENT IN PREHISTORIC TIMES*

ERASMUS MACMASTER
(1806-1866) President of Miami University of Ohio COULD REPLACE ANY PROFESSOR IN THE SCHOOL, TEACHING WITHOUT NOTES OR TEXTBOOK *-BECAUSE HE HAD MEMORIZED THE CONTENTS OF ENTIRE TEXTBOOKS ON EVERY SUBJECT TAUGHT AT THE UNIVERSITY*

GODOLPHIN ARABIAN
ONE OF THE 3 HORSES FROM WHICH
ALL THOROUGHBREDS ARE DESCENDANTS
ACCIDENTALLY KICKED TO DEATH A CAT
THAT SHARED ITS STABLE AND
SHORTLY AFTERWARD DIED ITSELF
–HAVING REFUSED EVER AGAIN
TO EITHER EAT OR DRINK

DINARDO BEETLES
ARE SO NIMBLE
THEY CAN SAFELY
MAKE THEIR HOME
*INSIDE AN ANTS'
NEST*

THE **CORPSE** THAT WAS EXECUTED
FOR TREASON (1604)
NICHOLAS L'HOSTE, a French spy,
REALIZING ESCAPE WAS IMPOSSIBLE
DROWNED HIMSELF IN THE MARNE
*HIS EMBALMED BODY WAS PUT ON TRIAL,
CONVICTED, AND PUBLICLY QUARTERED BY 4 HORSES*

THE **LIGHTHOUSE** on Tybee Island, Georgia, BUILT IN 1648
SERVED WITHOUT A LIGHT OF ANY KIND FOR 142 YEARS
IT WAS MERELY A DAYTIME WARNING UNTIL 1790

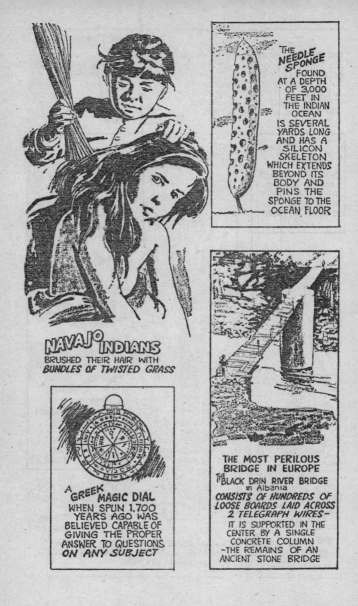

THE NEEDLE SPONGE FOUND AT A DEPTH OF 3,000 FEET IN THE INDIAN OCEAN IS SEVERAL YARDS LONG AND HAS A SILICON SKELETON WHICH EXTENDS BEYOND ITS BODY AND PINS THE SPONGE TO THE OCEAN FLOOR

NAVAJO INDIANS BRUSHED THEIR HAIR WITH *BUNDLES OF TWISTED GRASS*

A GREEK MAGIC DIAL WHEN SPUN 1,700 YEARS AGO WAS BELIEVED CAPABLE OF GIVING THE PROPER ANSWER TO QUESTIONS *ON ANY SUBJECT*

THE MOST PERILOUS BRIDGE IN EUROPE THE BLACK DRIN RIVER BRIDGE in Albania *CONSISTS OF HUNDREDS OF LOOSE BOARDS LAID ACROSS 2 TELEGRAPH WIRES—* IT IS SUPPORTED IN THE CENTER BY A SINGLE CONCRETE COLUMN —THE REMAINS OF AN ANCIENT STONE BRIDGE

AN ELEPHANT

CARVED IN NEW DELHI, INDIA, FROM
A SINGLE PIECE OF IVORY—
ALL THE DECORATIVE FEATURES
INCLUDING THE BLANKET,
CHAIN, PENDANT AND
BELLS SWING FREELY
*—YET ARE STILL ATTACHED TO
THE BODY OF THE ELEPHANT*

THE OFFICER WHOSE DEATH SENTENCE WON HIM A PROMOTION

*COLONEL BEAUMONT DE
LA BONNIERE (1760-1830)*
SENTENCED TO DEATH IN
LYON, FRANCE, IN 1792, FOR
CRITICIZING THE REVOLUTION,
WAS RESCUED ON HIS WAY TO
THE GUILLOTINE BY SOLDIERS
OF HIS COMMAND—WHO FORCED
*OFFICIALS TO PROMOTE THE
COLONEL TO THE RANK OF
BRIGADIER GENERAL*

A CENTURIES-OLD TREE

near Kriegenbrunn, Germany,
IS THE COMMUNITY'S MONUMENT
TO ITS WAR DEAD

A STONE SUNFLOWER

CARVED BY NATURE
in Mammoth Cave, Ky.

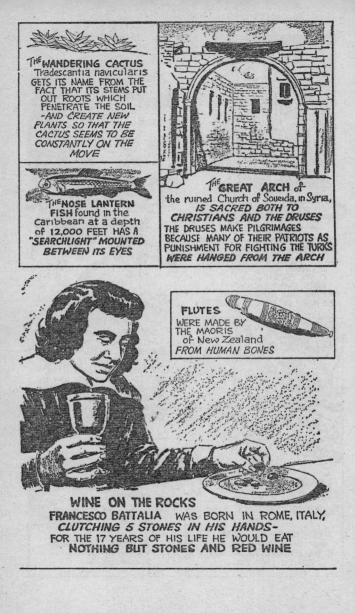

THE **WANDERING CACTUS** Tradescantia navicularis GETS ITS NAME FROM THE FACT THAT ITS STEMS PUT OUT ROOTS WHICH PENETRATE THE SOIL -AND CREATE NEW PLANTS SO THAT THE CACTUS SEEMS TO BE CONSTANTLY ON THE MOVE

THE **NOSE LANTERN FISH** found in the Caribbean at a depth of 12,000 FEET HAS A "SEARCHLIGHT" MOUNTED BETWEEN ITS EYES

THE **GREAT ARCH** of the ruined Church of Soueida, in Syria, *IS SACRED BOTH TO CHRISTIANS AND THE DRUSES* THE DRUSES MAKE PILGRIMAGES BECAUSE MANY OF THEIR PATRIOTS AS PUNISHMENT FOR FIGHTING THE TURKS *WERE HANGED FROM THE ARCH*

FLUTES WERE MADE BY THE MAORIS of New Zealand *FROM HUMAN BONES*

WINE ON THE ROCKS FRANCESCO BATTALIA WAS BORN IN ROME, ITALY, *CLUTCHING 5 STONES IN HIS HANDS*- FOR THE 17 YEARS OF HIS LIFE HE WOULD EAT **NOTHING BUT STONES AND RED WINE**

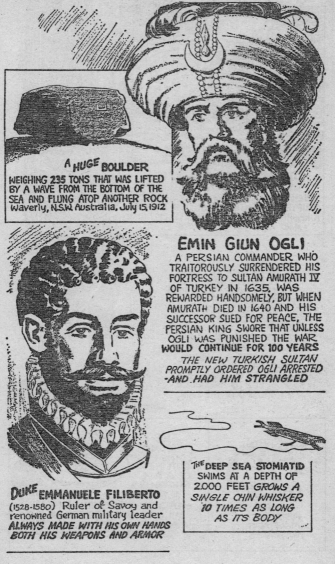

A HUGE BOULDER
WEIGHING 235 TONS THAT WAS LIFTED
BY A WAVE FROM THE BOTTOM OF THE
SEA AND FLUNG ATOP ANOTHER ROCK
Waverly, N.S.W. Australia, July 15, 1912

EMIN GIUN OGLI
A PERSIAN COMMANDER WHO
TRAITOROUSLY SURRENDERED HIS
FORTRESS TO SULTAN AMURATH IV
OF TURKEY IN 1635, WAS
REWARDED HANDSOMELY, BUT WHEN
AMURATH DIED IN 1640 AND HIS
SUCCESSOR SUED FOR PEACE, THE
PERSIAN KING SWORE THAT UNLESS
OGLI WAS PUNISHED THE WAR
WOULD CONTINUE FOR 100 YEARS
*THE NEW TURKISH SULTAN
PROMPTLY ORDERED OGLI ARRESTED
-AND HAD HIM STRANGLED*

DUKE EMMANUELE FILIBERTO
(1528-1580) Ruler of Savoy and
renowned German military leader
*ALWAYS MADE WITH HIS OWN HANDS
BOTH HIS WEAPONS AND ARMOR*

THE DEEP SEA STOMIATID
SWIMS AT A DEPTH OF
2,000 FEET *GROWS A
SINGLE CHIN WHISKER
10 TIMES AS LONG
AS ITS BODY*

THE YOUNGEST VOLCANO
SHOWA SHINZAN in Japan
WHICH BEGAN TO FORM IN DEC. 1943,
ERUPTED 6 MONTHS LATER WHEN IT REACHED
A HEIGHT OF 656 FEET, IS NOW 1,337 FEET HIGH
- *AND IS STILL GROWING*

THE **SEXTON**
of St. Martin's Church,
in Basel, Switzerland,
FOR CENTURIES HAS BEEN
REWARDED FOR RINGING
THE CHURCH BELL TO
ANNOUNCE THE OPENING OF
THE ANNUAL AUTUMN FAIR
*BY RECEIVING A GLOVE
FOR HIS LEFT HAND.*
HE GETS THE MATCHING
RIGHT GLOVE ONLY
WHEN HE PEALS THE
BELL TO ANNOUNCE
THE END OF THE FAIR

**PRESTWICHIA
AQUATICA**
IS A FLY
-*YET THE
MALE HAS
NO WINGS*

AN **EGG**
BEARING
THE
OUTLINE
OF A FOX
STRANGLING
A HEN
- LAID BY A CHICKEN A FEW
MINUTES AFTER ITS RESCUE BY
A FARMER IN BADEN, GERMANY, FROM
A FOX THAT WAS STRANGLING IT

NATIVES of Papua, New Guinea, SWIMMING UNDERWATER CATCH FISH WITH THEIR HANDS

THE GREAT MONOLITH in Red Canons Park near Canon City, Colo., 100 FEET HIGH HAS 4 DISTINCT HUMAN PROFILES

EDWIN BARKER of So. Haven, Mich., AT THE AGE OF 88 BOWLS 6 NIGHTS A WEEK —IN 7 DIFFERENT LEAGUES

DR. JOSEPH BELL (1837-1911) an Edinburgh surgeon *INSPIRED CONAN DOYLE TO CREATE SHERLOCK HOLMES—* DR. BELL, WHO WAS CONSULTED FREQUENTLY BY POLICE WHILE PRESIDENT OF THE ROYAL COLLEGE OF SURGEONS, WAS UNHAPPY OVER DOYLE'S WRITINGS—*BECAUSE HE PREFERRED TO BE KNOWN FOR HIS MEDICAL ABILITY*

THE **TWIN CHURCHES OF ST. ULRICH** Augsburg, Germany, 2 CHURCHES OF THE SAME NAME WHICH STAND SIDE BY SIDE — ONE A CATHOLIC CHURCH COMPLETED IN 1603 AND THE OTHER A PROTESTANT CHURCH, OPENED IN 1710

RESTAURANT DINERS in Zahle, a resort town in Lebanon, *SIT AT TABLES THAT STRADDLE BRANCHES OF THE BARDUNI RIVER*

THE **NEST** of the Beard Aztec Ant of Brazil CONSISTS OF THIN TUBES OF A CARD-BOARD-LIKE SUBSTANCE WHICH HANG FROM THE BRANCHES OF A TREE *LIKE A GIANT'S BEARD*

ERMINE in Ireland STAGE ELABORATE FUNERALS — OFTEN WITH PROCESSIONS OF UP TO 100 "MOURNERS" AND 4 "PALLBEARERS" *CARRYING THE BODY OF THE DEAD ERMINE*

ELEPHANT SKULL BOULEVARD in Gao, Sudan, Africa, IS LINED WITH STONE PYLONS —ATOP EACH OF WHICH IS THE SKULL OF AN ELEPHANT

BURGHAUSEN CASTLE THE LARGEST IN ALL GERMANY *IS 3,300 FEET WIDE*

A **KEROSENE LAMP** WAS LIT IN A WINDOW OF THE KEMP HOME IN A WOODED AREA IN Kerikeri, N.Z., BY 3 SUCCESSIVE GENERATIONS OF THE FAMILY —A SPAN OF 132 YEARS— THE HOUSE STILL DISPLAYS AN ELECTRIC LIGHT IN THE WINDOW TO GUIDE TRAVELERS

A CARINARIA MARINE SNAIL OVER A PERIOD OF THOUSANDS OF YEARS HAS CONVERTED THE SINGLE FOOT IT USED IN SWIMMING *INTO A VERTICAL FIN*

CHRISTMAS TREES ARE ERECTED AND ILLUMINATED ON CHRISTMAS NIGHT IN THE CEMETERIES OF BAVARIA *SO THE SOULS OF THE DEPARTED WILL NOT MISS THE YULE OBSERVANCE*

SALIS de SAGLIA A PARISIAN BOOTBLACK, WHO ALSO SERVED AS A MODEL FOR PICASSO, WAS SUCH AN ADMIRER OF PAUL VERLAINE, THE FRENCH POET, *THAT HE WORE ONE OF VERLAINE'S DISCARDED SHIRTS EVERY DAY FOR 5 YEARS —* HE NEVER LAUNDERED IT LEST THE SHIRT LOSE THE POET'S PERSONAL TOUCH

THE CARRIER SHELL a New Zealand shellfish CAMOUFLAGES ITSELF BY CEMENTING BITS OF ROCK AND SHELL TO ITS BACK

THE MISTLETOE TREE of Australia
WHICH RISES TO A HEIGHT OF 30 FEET, IS A PARASITE GROWING ON THE ROOTS OF OTHER PLANTS BURIED IN THE GROUND— IT BURSTS INTO FLOWER AT CHRISTMAS TIME AND IS USED IN AUSTRALIA AS A CHRISTMAS TREE

JOHANNES BRAHMS (1833-1897) PLAYED THE PIANO IN AN ALL-NIGHT SAILORS' DIVE IN HAMBURG, GERMANY, WHEN HE WAS 13 YEARS OF AGE—PLAYING EVERY TUNE FROM MEMORY WHILE READING A BOOK OF POETRY PROPPED UP ON HIS MUSIC RACK

REINDEER ARE SO VITAL TO THE CHUKCHIS, of Siberia, THAT THEIR LANGUAGE HAS 26 WORDS FOR REINDEER

THE "BEWITCHED TREE" on Great Comoro Island, in the Indian Ocean, IS BELIEVED BY NATIVES TO HAVE THE POWER — IF A SPELL COULD BE REMOVED FROM ITS BRANCHES— TO POINT OUT THE HIDING PLACE OF BURIED TREASURE

THE HERMIT OF MEREDITH
New Hampshire
JOSEPH PLUMMER (1774-1862) JILTED BY
THE GIRL HE LOVED, WAS SO DETERMINED TO
RENOUNCE THE WORLD THAT HE SPENT 70
YEARS IN A CABIN WITHOUT WINDOWS

FORTRESSES erected by the
village of Iconi, on
the Great Comoro Islands
in the Indian Ocean,
AS PROTECTION AGAINST
MADAGASCAR PIRATES, WERE
*SHAPED LIKE PROFILES
OF THE PIRATES' IDOLS*

ROUND BULLBOATS used by Plains Indians on the Missouri River
WERE MADE OF BUFFALO HIDE AND PROPELLED BY
HOLDING ONTO THE TAIL OF A SWIMMING HORSE

THE **STINGBULL** fish HAS POISONOUS STINGS IN ITS FINS AND GILLS - YET FISHERMEN CONSIDER IT AN EXCELLENT EATING FISH

DOLMENS
THE GREAT TOMBSTONES BUILT IN EUROPE IN PREHISTORIC TIMES FOR TRIBAL LEADERS, EACH HAD A LARGE "DOORWAY" *SO THE DECEASED'S SOUL COULD COME AND GO*

SILVER MINT
WON THE 1949 JUMPING EVENT ON THE WHITE CITY TRACK, IN LONDON, ENGLAND, *WHEN THE HORSE WAS 28 YEARS OF AGE* ITS RIDER, ALAN OLIVER, WAS ONLY IT

THE FROG FISH
which inhabits the weed-choked Sargasso Sea
LOOKS EXACTLY LIKE THE WEEDS AMONG WHICH IT DWELLS

MOSS GROWING ON A WALL IN THE PERFECT OUTLINE OF POPEYE'S FRIEND *WIMPY*

FIELD MARSHAL de La BOURDONNAYE (1747-1793) of France HAD NO FIRST NAME *UNTIL HE WAS 30 YEARS OF AGE* HE HAD AN AILING OLDER BROTHER WHO WAS EXPECTED TO DIE AND HIS PARENTS WANTED TO GIVE HIM HIS BROTHER'S NAME - BUT HE WAS OUTLIVED BY HIS BROTHER

THE OLD STONE HOUSE in Morgantown, W.Va., BUILT IN 1795 AS A DWELLING, SUCCESSIVELY SERVED AS A *POTTERY, TAVERN, TAILOR SHOP, TANNERY, CHURCH AND JUNK SHOP* -IT IS NOW A THRIFT SHOP OPERATED FOR CHARITY

THE **OXALIS PLANT** FOLDS UP ITS LEAVES WHEN IT IS COLD AND ON SUNNY DAYS IT FOLDS UP ITS FLOWERS

MANY TYPES OF DESERT ANTS CARRY THEIR DEAD TO ANT CEMETERIES

THE **CUPOLA** of the Church of the Jesuits, in Vienna, Austria **IS NOT A CUPOLA AT ALL** IT IS AN OPTICAL ILLUSION, PAINTED ON A VERTICAL FLAT SURFACE BY ANDREA POZZO, IN 1703, TO ILLUSTRATE HIS THEORIES ON PERSPECTIVE

CORMORANTS on the islands of Albemarle and Narborough in the Galapagos Archipelago of Ecuador **ARE THE ONLY ONES IN THE WORLD THAT *CANNOT FLY***

THE LONG STAIRWAY on the century-old house in Mobile, Ala., ORIGINALLY LED DIRECTLY TO THE SIDEWALK BUT IT WAS SWITCHED TO THE SIDE OF THE PORCH BY A MOTHER WHO FEARED PASSING GENTLEMEN WOULD **GLIMPSE HER DAUGHTER'S ANKLES**

THE **FIRST WOMAN TO USE FACE POWDER** MARGUERITE de VALOIS (1553-1615) Queen of Navarre SUFFERING FROM ECZEMA AT THE AGE OF 53 USED RICE POWDER TO HIDE HER BLEMISHES *- AND LAUNCHED A FEMININE FASHION*

A VILLAGE OF THE NARAVUTE TRIBE,
IN THE NORTHWESTERN AMAZON AREA OF S.A.
OFTEN CONSISTS OF A SINGLE DWELLING
- INHABITED BY 100 MEMBERS
OF THE SAME FAMILY

EMPEROR
NINTOKU
TENNO (289-399)
WHO LIVED TO
THE AGE OF 110
RULED JAPAN
FOR A PERIOD
OF 86 YEARS

THE FIRST PROFESSIONAL MOURNER
THE DRUMMER of the
Grenadier Guard Regiment of Prussia
BY ORDER OF KING FREDERICK THE GREAT
THROUGHOUT THE SEVEN YEARS WAR
AGAINST AUSTRIA AND RUSSIA
WAS SEVERELY WHIPPED WHENEVER
A GRENADIER WAS KILLED
THIS MADE CERTAIN THAT AT
LEAST ONE MAN WOULD CRY
FOR EACH FALLEN COMRADE (1756-1763)

A KING PINE TREE
on the banks of the Huon River, N.Z.,
PUT OUT ROOTS THAT STRADDLED
THE TRUNK OF A FALLEN PINE
THAT HAD GROWN ON THE SAME
SPOT FOR 1,045 YEARS

THE ISLAND CREATED BY THROWING ROCKS

CHISEL ISLAND in the Gulf of Kotor, Yugoslavia, ORIGINALLY WAS ONLY A SMALL ROCK PROJECTING ABOVE THE WATER TO ENLARGE IT TO ACCOMMODATE A CHURCH, NATIVES THREW STONES INTO THE WATER FOR 150 YEARS

SIR JOHN ELDON GORST (1835-1916) of Waikato County, N.Z., FROM 1860 TO 1863 HELD EVERY CIVIL SERVICE POST IN THE COUNTRY —SIMULTANEOUSLY SERVING AS POSTMASTER, CUSTOMS OFFICIAL, HARBOR MASTER, MAGISTRATE AND POLICEMAN

THE FLYING DRAGON IS A LIZARD THAT CAN SOAR FROM TREE TO TREE

THE FIRST "PUBLISHED" WORK OF THE FAMOUS GERMAN AUTHOR GOETHE WAS A WINE LABEL

THE REV. **SALOMON BRENNWALD**
(1637-1706) of Stammheim, Switzerland,
HAS ON HIS TOMBSTONE
THIS EPITAPH:
HE WAS THE MINISTER OF
3 PARISHES, 3 TIMES A
DEAN, MARRIED 3 TIMES,
HAD 3 CHILDREN BY
EACH OF HIS FIRST
TWO WIVES, 3 BOYS
AND 3 GIRLS-LIVED
TO THE AGE OF 3 TIMES
23 AND IS BURIED IN
TRINITY CHURCHYARD

UNFAIR

FEMALE BABIES
ARE IGNORED
IN THE FRENCH
LANGUAGE
BÉBÉ, THE
FRENCH WORD FOR
BABY, IS MALE

THE **PRUDHOMME HOUSE** in Natchitoches, La.,
HAS A SEPARATE OUTSIDE
ENTRANCE FOR EVERY ROOM
EACH GUEST WAS GIVEN HIS OWN
LATCHKEY AND COULD GO AND COME WITHOUT
DISTURBING OTHERS IN THE HOUSE

CANADA THISTLE
A WEED
SPREADS UNDERGROUND
ITS ROOTS BURROW THROUGH
THE SOIL HORIZONTALLY AT
A DEPTH OF 2 FEET, AND
SEND UP NEW PLANTS
AT INTERVALS

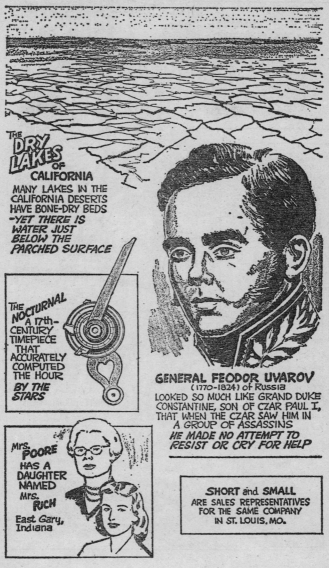

THE DRY LAKES OF CALIFORNIA

MANY LAKES IN THE CALIFORNIA DESERTS HAVE BONE-DRY BEDS —YET THERE IS WATER JUST BELOW THE PARCHED SURFACE

THE NOCTURNAL
A 17th-CENTURY TIMEPIECE THAT ACCURATELY COMPUTED THE HOUR BY THE STARS

GENERAL FEODOR UVAROV
(1770-1824) of Russia
LOOKED SO MUCH LIKE GRAND DUKE CONSTANTINE, SON OF CZAR PAUL I, THAT WHEN THE CZAR SAW HIM IN A GROUP OF ASSASSINS HE MADE NO ATTEMPT TO RESIST OR CRY FOR HELP

Mrs. POORE HAS A DAUGHTER NAMED Mrs. RICH
East Gary, Indiana

SHORT and SMALL
ARE SALES REPRESENTATIVES FOR THE SAME COMPANY IN ST. LOUIS, MO.

THE **CHICHAMAYA**
A DANCE PERFORMED BY THE GOAJIRO TRIBE OF VENEZUELA, REQUIRES THE MAN TO BACK UP RAPIDLY IN A NARROW CIRCLE WHILE HIS FEMALE PARTNER DANCES FORWARD *-AND ATTEMPTS TO TRIP HIM UP*

ATTILA'S THRONE
on the island of Torcello, off Venice, Italy,

A BLOCK OF MARBLE USED AS A THRONE BY THE KING OF THE HUNS *1,514 YEARS AGO*

THE **MAN** WHOSE LIFE WAS SAVED BECAUSE HE WAS BITTERLY HATED

DAVIT BECK (1621-1656) FAMED DUTCH COURT PAINTER WHO WOULD NEVER PERMIT WINE TO TOUCH HIS LIPS *WAS PRONOUNCED DEAD IN 1647*

HIS SERVANTS, BITTER AGAINST THEIR TYRANNICAL MASTER, POURED WINE INTO THE CORPSE'S MOUTH *- AND HE REVIVED!*

A PAINTING of *ST. BERNARD* BY AN OLD FLEMISH MASTER DONATED TO THE NATIONAL GALLERY OF ART, IN WASHINGTON, D.C., *WAS FOUND TO HAVE ANOTHER MASTERPIECE ON THE BACK COVERED WITH A COAT OF BLACK PAINT*

THE *WOOL* ON A SHEEP GROWS FASTER IN SUMMER THAN IN WINTER

THE MAN WHO WATCHED HIS OWN FUNERAL

NICOLAS HEYENDAL (1658-1733) of Walhorn, Belgium,

AFTER HAVING BEEN KIDNAPED BY PIRATES *WANDERED INTO A CHURCH AND WITNESSED A FUNERAL—*

HE SUDDENLY REALIZED THAT HIS MOTHER HAD MISTAKENLY IDENTIFIED THE BODY OF A VAGRANT AS THAT OF HER OWN SON —AND THE FUNERAL WAS HIS OWN!

WOMEN of Eastern Macedonia CELEBRATE EACH JAN. 7th AS THEIR DAY OF INDEPENDENCE, ASSEMBLING IN COFFEE HOUSES FOR GAY PARTIES WHILE THEIR *HUSBANDS CLEAN THE HOUSE, COOK DINNER AND MAKE THE BEDS*

PIERRE BOUGUER (1698-1758) French mathematician GAVE INSTRUCTION TO HIS MATHEMATICS PROFESSOR WHEN *HE WAS A STUDENT 13 YEARS OF AGE* —AT 15 HE WAS HIMSELF AN ACCREDITED PROFESSOR

THE JAWS OF EVERY PIG SLAUGHTERED ON THE ISLAND OF NIAS, SUMATRA, MUST BE KEPT FOREVER SUSPENDED ON HOOKS IN THE HOUSES IN WHICH THE ANIMALS WERE EATEN *—TO INSURE THE SALVATION OF EACH PIG'S SOUL*

THE **DEVIL'S WINDMILL**
near Guérande, France,
IS SO CALLED BECAUSE ITS
OWNER, YVES KERBIC, INSISTED
THAT IN EXCHANGE FOR HIS SOUL
*THE DEVIL HELPED HIM BUILD
IT IN A SINGLE NIGHT*

ARTHUR YOUNG (1741-1820)
an English agriculturist
MADE A 3-MONTH HORSEBACK
RIDE ACROSS FRANCE IN 1788
- *RIDING A MARE THAT
WAS TOTALLY BLIND*

JEFFERSON'S SALAMANDERS
DIE BY THE
THOUSANDS
IN THE LARVA
STAGE BECAUSE
THE PARENTS
ALWAYS LAY
THEIR EGGS IN
SMALL PUDDLES
OF WATER
WHICH DRY
UP BEFORE
THE LARVAE
HAVE HAD
TIME TO
DEVELOP

THE **WATER RANUNCULUS**
PLANT HAS NORMAL
LEAVES ABOVE THE WATER
- *BUT ITS UNDERWATER
LEAVES LOOK LIKE
RIBBONS*

A **PESSIMIST'S TIMEPIECE**
THAT COMPRISES BOTH A *WATCH AND AN HOURGLASS*
IF ONE FAILS, THE OTHER CAN BE USED

THE **DOUBLE BRIDGE**
in Paris, France, IS SO CALLED BECAUSE IN THE 17th CENTURY THE TOLL PERMITTING A MAN ON HORSEBACK TO CROSS IT WAS A **DOUBLE LIVRE (48¢)**
FOR 187 YEARS THE BRIDGE'S TOLLS PROVIDED THE ENTIRE FINANCIAL SUPPORT FOR THE ST. LOUIS HOSPITAL

THE **OLD MAN'S BEARD**
a Brazilian plant THAT GROWS WITHOUT ROOTS ON THE BRANCHES OF TREES IS USED BY BIRDS IN BUILDING THEIR NESTS -BUT IT SPREADS SO RAPIDLY IT DRIVES THE BIRDS OUT OF THE NEST

THE **PRESCRIPTION PAGODA!**
Seoul, Korea
A *PORTABLE MARBLE PAGODA* WAS SHIPPED IN **2** SECTIONS FROM PEIPING, CHINA, ON THE ADVICE OF A PHYSICIAN TO SAVE THE LIFE OF PRINCESS PAZLA- -WHO WAS HOMESICK FOR HER NATIVE CHINA (1352)

THE STEEPEST STAIRWAY
THE *STAIRS* between High Town, and Lower Town, in Bar-le-Duc, France, RISE SO ABRUPTLY THAT THEY ZIGZAG FROM ONE STREET TO ANOTHER *SO THE CLIMBER WON'T SUFFER FROM VERTIGO*

WHALEBONE **WAR CLUBS** used by the Maori of New Zealand WERE ELABORATELY CARVED IN THE BELIEF THAT THE FANCIER THE CARVING THE MORE *EFFECTIVE THEY WOULD BE IN BATTLE*

"108" IS THE FULL NAME OF A HINDU HOLY MAN *INDICATING HE HAS CONQUERED ALL 108 SINS THAT TEMPT EVERY HINDU MALE* Amarnath, India

THE **EARL OF LONSDALE** (1857-1944) DID NOT ONCE MISS A RUNNING OF THE ENGLISH DERBY *IN 62 YEARS*

FUNERAL URNS USED BY THE ANCIENT ETRUSCANS of Italy TO HOLD THE ASHES OF DEPARTED KIN WERE SHAPED LIKE THE HOUSES THEY OCCUPIED IN LIFE —*TO MAKE THE SOULS FEEL AT HOME*

JOHANN OSTLER A MOUNTAIN GUIDE WHO CLIMBED THE 9,728-FOOT ZUGSPITZE, GERMANY'S HIGHEST PEAK, 500 TIMES, DIED IN 1897 AFTER HURTING HIMSELF *CHOPPING WOOD*

THE HARP TREE A TRIPLE-TRUNKED BEECH Johanniskreuz, Germany

THE CLICK BEETLE WHICH ACTUALLY HAS VERY SMALL EYES APPEARS TO BE WEARING AN ENORMOUS PAIR OF GOGGLES OVER 2 GIANT EYES

THE GUESTHOUSE OF THE GODS Island of Bali, Indonesia, AN 11-STORY HOTEL ON THE SHORES OF LAKE BRATAN TO ACCOMMODATE THE GODS FOR OVERNIGHT STAYS

THE INDIAN FOUNTAIN ERECTED IN Mt. Kisco, N.Y., IN 1907 DESIGNED FOR WATERING HORSES, BEARS THE INSCRIPTION: "God's only beverage for man and beast"

THE TUFTED BEETLE IS SHELTERED AND FED BY ANTS —WHICH IT REPAYS BY FEEDING ON YOUNG ANTS

TREES ON A HORSE FARM IN Babolna, Hungary, HAVE THEIR FOLIAGE TRIMMED TO FORM THE PROFILES OF PREVIOUS MANAGERS OF THE FARM

IRON BOOMERANGS USED BY THE NIAM-NIAM TRIBE of Africa HAVE 3 SHARP BLADES SO THAT *THEY ALWAYS HIT WITH A CUTTING BLOW*

THE BEARDED CHILDREN OF INDIA

THE TODAS CELEBRATE A BIRTHDAY ONLY ONCE IN EVERY 7 YEARS—

A MAN WITH A BUSHY BEARD MAY BE ONLY 3 YEARS OF AGE

THE WEDDING WELLS

3 WELLS are located side by side on Mykonos, Greece, AND IT IS A TRADITION THAT A MALE VISITOR WHO DRINKS FROM ALL THREE *WILL MARRY A GIRL FROM MYKONOS*

A PAIR OF EYEGLASSES WORN BY ST. PHILIP 371 YEARS AGO—
THEY ARE PRESERVED IN THE CHURCH OF SAINT PHILIP DE NERI IN ROME, ITALY

THE **ARCOLE BRIDGE** in Paris, France, IS NAMED IN HONOR OF A LOCKSMITH WHO STORMED IT DURING THE FRENCH REVOLUTION, SHOUTING: "REMEMBER ME, MY FRIENDS, MY NAME IS ARCOLE" (1830)

DR. **NICHOLAS HACKE**
(1800-1878)
BECAME PASTOR OF 5 CHURCHES IN DIFFERENT LOCALITIES IN PENNSYLVANIA AT THE AGE OF 19 AND CONTINUED TO COMMUTE BETWEEN THEM ON HORSEBACK FOR **59 YEARS**

AN **ISLAND**
400 FEET LONG AND 100 FEET WIDE APPEARED IN LAKE ZURICH, SWITZERLAND, ON MARCH 12, 1909
THEN DISAPPEARED THE VERY NEXT DAY AND HAS NEVER BEEN SEEN AGAIN

"ROXIE"
DOG MASCOT OF THE LONG ISLAND RAILROAD FOR 12 YEARS
HAD ATTACHED TO HIS COLLAR A PASS PERMITTING HIM UNLIMITED RIDING PRIVILEGES

THE FIRST ELECTRIC INCLINED RAILWAY
ECHO MOUNTAIN RAILWAY CARRYING PASSENGERS 3,000 FEET TO THE TOP OF ECHO MOUNTAIN, PASADENA, CALIF., WAS PUT INTO SERVICE JULY 4, 1893
-THE FIRST ELECTRIC INCLINED RAILWAY IN THE WORLD

EVERY GIRL
IN THE SHAIKH FAMILY of Shaikh Mand, Iraq, IS NAMED JAHERU—WHICH MEANS "SNAKE POISON" AND THEY ARE ALL IMMUNE TO THE BITE OF VENOMOUS SERPENTS

DOGWOOD TREE
SHAPED LIKE THE HEAD OF A DEER

TRIBAL COUNCILS RULED ANCIENT GERMAN COMMUNITIES, AND TO ASSURE WEIGHTY CONSIDERATION OF ALL LEGISLATION, EACH PROPOSAL HAD TO BE DISCUSSED AT TWO SUCCESSIVE SESSIONS -*THE FIRST WHILE THE COUNCIL MEMBERS WERE DRUNK AND THE SECOND WHEN THEY WERE SOBER*

The **ANTENNAE** of the male **Mecomastyx Weevil** ARE 8 TIMES AS LONG AS ITS ENTIRE BODY

SEAMUS BURKE A PROFESSIONAL MAGICIAN BOUND FROM HEAD TO FOOT AND CARRYING A SEALED TISSUE BAG OVER HIS SHOULDER, AFTER TWO MINUTES BEHIND A SCREEN WOULD REAPPEAR TO HIS AUDIENCE *INSIDE THE SEALED BAG*

MONKEY ON A TREE NATURAL FORMATION

THE URUSSU A BRAZILIAN HONEY BEE DARTS AGGRESSIVELY AT CREATURES OF ANY SIZE -YET IT HAS NO STING

WILLIAM R. WATSON of Alberta, Canada, HAS BEEN COMPLETELY PARALYZED IN BOTH HANDS SINCE BIRTH -YET HE SHAVES, DRESSES AND FEEDS HIMSELF, RIDES HORSEBACK AND SWIMS, ICE-SKATES, PLAYS HOCKEY AND CARDS AS A BOY HE HAD A NEWSPAPER ROUTE AND MOWED LAWNS, USING HIS FEET AS HANDS

THE MILLI-HOOP THE MILLIPEDE TO ESCAPE ENEMIES COILS INTO A HOOP AND ROLLS AWAY

THE BELFRY of the Cathedral of Torino, in Italy, WAS COMPLETED 30 YEARS BEFORE CONSTRUCTION OF THE CATHEDRAL ITSELF WAS EVEN STARTED

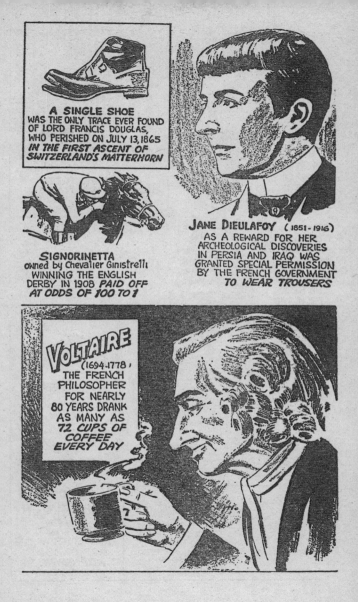

A SINGLE SHOE
WAS THE ONLY TRACE EVER FOUND OF LORD FRANCIS DOUGLAS, WHO PERISHED ON JULY 13, 1865 *IN THE FIRST ASCENT OF SWITZERLAND'S MATTERHORN*

SIGNORINETTA
owned by Chevalier Ginistrelli WINNING THE ENGLISH DERBY IN 1908 *PAID OFF AT ODDS OF 100 TO 1*

JANE DIEULAFOY (1851- 1916)
AS A REWARD FOR HER ARCHEOLOGICAL DISCOVERIES IN PERSIA AND IRAQ WAS GRANTED SPECIAL PERMISSION BY THE FRENCH GOVERNMENT *TO WEAR TROUSERS*

VOLTAIRE
(1694-1778)
THE FRENCH PHILOSOPHER FOR NEARLY 80 YEARS DRANK AS MANY AS *72 CUPS OF COFFEE EVERY DAY*

THE **EYES** THAT MUST NEVER "SEE" OXEN
THE SWAYAMBHUNATH TEMPLE of Nepal
HAS A PAIR OF EYES ON EACH OF ITS 4 SIDES, AND NO LAND THAT CAN BE SEEN FROM THE TEMPLE HAS BEEN CULTIVATED EXCEPT BY HAND *FOR 2,200 YEARS*

THE MAIN STREET of Barbotan, France, *RUNS RIGHT THROUGH THE TOWN'S CHURCH*

THE **SPHINX MOTH** HAS A TONGUE SO LONG THAT IT IS CARRIED COILED IN A TIGHT SPIRAL

W.E.TOWELLS WAS BORN IN *BATH,* ENGLAND, AND LIVES AT THE AGE OF 88 IN *HOT SPRINGS,* ARKANSAS

AN **OLD TRAIN**
CONSISTING OF A
LOCOMOTIVE, FLAT
CAR AND COACH
STANDS NEAR THE
OLD STATION IN
Central City, Colo.,
AS A MEMORIAL
TO A RAILWAY
LINE THAT
SERVED THE
AREA'S MINES
**90 YEARS
AGO**

A
CANNON
BALL THAT
WAS FIRED
FOR A
BALL

THE WATER IN THE Medici Fountain, IN Rome, Italy,
SPOUTS FROM A CANNON BALL THAT WAS
FIRED BY QUEEN CHRISTINA OF SWEDEN AGAINST
THE GATE OF THE VILLA MEDICI IN 1658
*TO REMIND INHABITANTS OF THE VILLA THEY
WERE INVITED TO THE EXILED QUEEN'S BALL*

**EVERY
CHILD**
IN Arenys de
Mar, Spain,
IS REQUIRED
TO WALK
THROUGH THE
STREETS EACH
DECEMBER 8th
*SMOKING
A PIPE*

FARMERS in the Maprik territory of New Guinea *ARE FORBIDDEN TO EAT PRODUCE FROM THEIR OWN LAND* EACH FARMER EXHIBITS HIS CROPS IN THE MARKET PLACE—AND THEN EXCHANGES HIS PRODUCE FOR THAT GROWN BY ANOTHER FARMER

COUNT MORIC SANDOR (1805-1878) A HUNGARIAN SPORTSMAN ARRIVED AT A DANCE ON THE SECOND FLOOR OF THE WHITE-SWAN INN IN BUDAPEST *BY RIDING UP THE STAIRWAY ON A HORSE*

THE LEAPING SHELL

A SPECIES OF MOLLUSK found in Australia HAS ONE MODIFIED LEG *ON WHICH IT MAKES GREAT LEAPS*

CATTLE in India CANNOT BE WORKED ON MONDAYS—YET INDIAN FARMERS HAVE NO DAY OF REST

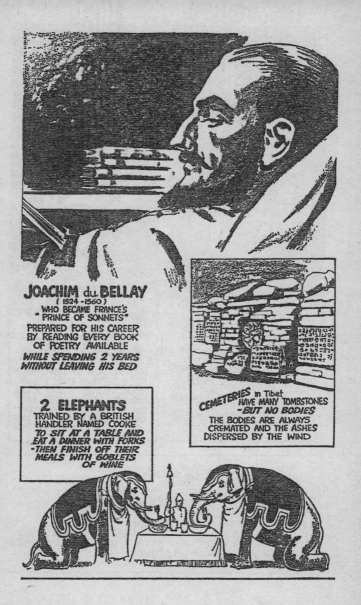

JOACHIM du BELLAY
(1524 -1560)
WHO BECAME FRANCE'S
"PRINCE OF SONNETS"

PREPARED FOR HIS CAREER
BY READING EVERY BOOK
OF POETRY AVAILABLE

*WHILE SPENDING 2 YEARS
WITHOUT LEAVING HIS BED*

CEMETERIES in Tibet
HAVE MANY TOMBSTONES
- BUT NO BODIES
THE BODIES ARE ALWAYS
CREMATED AND THE ASHES
DISPERSED BY THE WIND

2 ELEPHANTS
TRAINED BY A BRITISH
HANDLER NAMED COOKE
*TO SIT AT A TABLE AND
EAT A DINNER WITH FORKS
- THEN FINISH OFF THEIR
MEALS WITH GOBLETS
OF WINE*

The WOMAN CHASER
THE SECRET EWE SOCIETY
in Togo, Africa,
WHICH BARRED WOMEN UNDER
THREAT OF DEATH-ERECTED A
WOODEN SENTINEL AT THE DOORWAY
AND INSISTED THAT IF A WOMAN
IN DISGUISE PASSED IT
*THE CARVED GUARDIAN WOULD
ISSUE A DENOUNCING CRY*

The CHURCH OF CONTIGNY
in France
WAS STRUCK BY LIGHTNING
WHILE SERVICES WERE BEING
CONDUCTED IN IT ON JUNE 21,1789,
AND THE BELFRY CRASHED INTO
THE EDIFICE, DEMOLISHING THE
CHURCH-*YET NOT ONE OF THE
153 WORSHIPERS WAS INJURED*

A SPECIAL TALLY STICK
used by the Kei Islanders of Malaya
WHO-PURCHASE THEIR WIVES WHEN THE GIRLS ARE BABIES AND
INSERT A MARKER IN THE TALLY STICK TO RECORD EACH PAYMENT
MADE OVER A PERIOD OF 20 YEARS

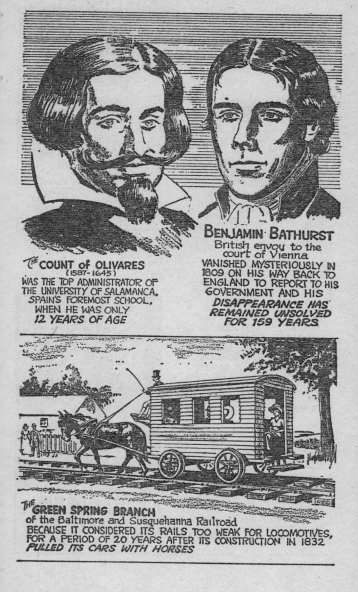

THE COUNT of OLIVARES
(1587-1645)
WAS THE TOP ADMINISTRATOR OF
THE UNIVERSITY OF SALAMANCA,
SPAIN'S FOREMOST SCHOOL,
WHEN HE WAS ONLY
12 YEARS OF AGE

Benjamin Bathurst
British envoy to the
court of Vienna
VANISHED MYSTERIOUSLY IN
1809 ON HIS WAY BACK TO
ENGLAND TO REPORT TO HIS
GOVERNMENT AND HIS
*DISAPPEARANCE HAS
REMAINED UNSOLVED
FOR 159 YEARS*

THE GREEN SPRING BRANCH
of the Baltimore and Susquehanna Railroad
BECAUSE IT CONSIDERED ITS RAILS TOO WEAK FOR LOCOMOTIVES,
FOR A PERIOD OF 20 YEARS AFTER ITS CONSTRUCTION IN 1832
PULLED ITS CARS WITH HORSES

FARM BUILDINGS
at Voss, Norway,
ARE BUILT AGAINST THE MOUNTAIN
WITH THEIR ROOFS PITCHED
IN LINE WITH ITS SLOPE SO
*THE FREQUENT AVALANCHES WILL
ROAR HARMLESSLY OVER THEM*

THE **STRANGEST GAMBLE**
IN HISTORY

Professor Francisco Garrido
COMPLETING A LECTURE AT THE
SCHOOL OF PHYSIOLOGY AND
HYGIENE, IN MADRID, SPAIN,
ANNOUNCED HE WAS RESIGNING
HIS POST TO PURCHASE A
POPULAR PHARMACY WITH HIS
WINNINGS IN A NATIONAL LOTTERY
*—THE DRAWING FOR WHICH
HAD NOT YET BEEN HELD!*

HIS TICKET WON AND HE
BECAME THE WEALTHIEST
PHARMACIST IN THE COUNTRY
(1870)

VINLAND
THE VIKING NAME
FOR NEW ENGLAND
IS MENTIONED IN VIKING WRITING
CARVED IN 1065 ON A STONE
FOUND IN HOENEN, NORWAY—
*IT REPORTS A VIKING JOURNEY
TO VINLAND IN 985*

THE **GROTTO** of the **TWO FLAGS**
in the Cave of Hötl-Loch, Switzerland,
HAS ON ITS WALL 2 HUGE
STALACTITES SHAPED LIKE
FLUTTERING FLAGS

THE TUAREGS OF THE SAHARA DESERT STILL FIGHT DUELS *USING MEDIEVAL WEAPONS AND SHIELDS*

DENIS DIDEROT (1713-1784) a French author

TO PROVIDE A DOWRY FOR HIS DAUGHTER SOLD HIS LIBRARY TO EMPRESS CATHERINE II of Russia FOR $3,000 AND CONTRACTED TO SERVE AS CUSTODIAN OF THE LIBRARY FOR 50 YEARS AT AN ANNUAL SALARY OF $200

THE EMPRESS INSISTED THAT THE ENTIRE SALARY BE PAID TO HIM IN ADVANCE

POPCORN WHEN POPPED EXPANDS AS MUCH AS **27** TIMES ITS ORIGINAL SIZE

"REGRET" WAS THE ONLY FILLY THAT EVER WON THE KENTUCKY DERBY SHE DID IT IN 1915

THE ANT APE BEETLE
TO DISCOURAGE PREDATORS LOOKS AND BEHAVES LIKE AN ANT

AUSTRALIAN ABORIGINES
USE TENDRILS OF A TOUGH VINE AS FISHHOOKS

THE POET WHOSE MANUSCRIPT WAS A FOREST
MACIEJ SARBIEWSKI (1595-1640) THE POLISH POET WHO WROTE IN LATIN, SPURNED THE USE OF PEN AND PAPER
HE CARVED EACH POEM IN THE BARK OF OAK TREES IN A FOREST NEAR KRAZEJ, LITHUANIA

THE STREET OF BEAUTIFUL WOMEN
in Caudebec, France, HAS HAD THAT NAME FOR 200 YEARS AND ITS RESIDENTS BOAST
THE MOST BEAUTIFUL WOMEN IN THE TOWN HAVE LIVED THERE ALL THAT TIME

THE QUARRION PARROT of Australia NEVER ENTERS ITS NEST WITHOUT FIRST TAKING A BATH

THE **CHURCH OF HAHNENKLEE** in Germany WAS BUILT WITHOUT USE OF A SINGLE NAIL
IT IS THE SCENE OF COUNTLESS WEDDINGS BECAUSE BRIDES BELIEVE THEY ARE ASSURED OF A SMOOTH BLENDING IN THEIR MARITAL LIVES

THE *YOUNGEST* **MURDERESS IN HISTORY** MARIETTE BANDET of Bouches-du-Rhone, France, STABBED TO DEATH HER 8-YEAR-OLD SISTER *WHEN SHE HERSELF WAS ONLY 2 YEARS OF AGE*

THE **ARCADE** BUILT IN PHILADELPHIA, PA., IN 1826, WAS AMERICA'S FIRST OFFICE BUILDING

BONE SHAPED LIKE AN *EAGLE IN FLIGHT*

THE THEATRE OF THE INDEPENDENTS in Rome, Italy, IS LOCATED IN AN ANCIENT ROMAN BATH

THE BRITISH LORD WHO COULDN'T READ OR WRITE

HENRY CLIFFORD (1455-1553) AN ENGLISH ORPHAN, CONDEMNED TO DEATH AT THE AGE OF 7 FOR HIS FATHER'S ACTS, ESCAPED AND WAS AN ILLITERATE SHEPHERD FOR 23 YEARS —BUT IN 1485 HE WAS RESTORED TO HIS RIGHTFUL PLACE AS 14TH LORD CLIFFORD, 10TH BARON WESTMORLAND, FIRST LORD VESCI, AND POSSESSOR OF ONE OF ENGLAND'S GREATEST FORTUNES!

THE OLD NORSEMAN - STONE FORMATION Baker's Island, Salem, Mass.

RABBIT WITH 3 HORNS shot by Randy Young, Jackson, Tenn.

THE **CHURCH OF ST. FRANCIS** LOCATED IN THE **LIGHTHOUSE** of Algarve, Portugal, IS COMPLETELY LINED *WITH HUMAN SKULLS AND BONES*

THE TREATMENT TREE
THE BHIL TRIBE of India BELIEVES THAT ANY CHILDHOOD DISEASE CAN BE INSTANTLY CURED *BY PASSING THE AILING INFANT 7 TIMES THROUGH THE NATURAL OPENING IN THE TRUNK OF A PALAS TREE*

A RIP IN A BATHROOM WALL CAUSED WHEN A TOWEL RACK WAS PULLED OFF *FORMED THE PERFECT OUTLINE OF A MAN'S HEAD*

THE UNDERWATER STATUE

CHRIST OF THE DEPTHS
A MEMORIAL HONORING
ITALIAN SOLDIERS DROWNED
ON THE ENGLISH TRANSPORT,
"CROESUS," WHICH SANK DURING
THE CRIMEAN WAR, IS LOCATED
OFF SAN FRUTTUOSO, ITALY, AT
THE BOTTOM OF THE LIGURIAN SEA
ITS BASE IS 60 FEET BELOW
THE SURFACE

A **METAL CHAIR**
WITH
5 TOADSTOOLS
GROWING
OUT OF IT

THE **COURTHOUSE**
of Box Butte County, Neb.,
WHEN THE COUNTY SEAT WAS
MOVED FROM HEMINGFORD TO
ALLIANCE SOME 80 YEARS AGO
*WAS SHIFTED TO ITS NEW
LOCATION ON A FLATCAR*

THE GRAMPUS CAN SWALLOW A SEAL WHOLE AND THEN DISGORGE THE SKIN – WHICH HAS BEEN MYSTERIOUSLY REMOVED IN THE STOMACH OF THE GRAMPUS

THE RICE BIRD OFTEN GORGES ITSELF ON SO MUCH RICE THAT IF IT IS SHOT BY A HUNTER ITS BODY BURSTS WHEN IT HITS THE GROUND

KING PHILIP II (1527-1598) of Spain FEARING THAT A CANAL ACROSS PANAMA WOULD ENDANGER SPANISH AMERICA MADE IT AN OFFENSE PUNISHABLE BY DEATH TO EVEN MENTION SUCH A PROJECT THE BAN WAS IN EFFECT FOR 201 YEARS

CHURCHES on the Faeroe Islands STAND IN YARDS OVERGROWN WITH LUSH GRASS THERE IS A SEVERE SHORTAGE OF GRASS FOR THE ISLANDS' ANIMALS, BUT THE CHURCHYARD GRASS, WHEN HARVESTED, ALWAYS IS THROWN INTO THE SEA

FRIENDS GREET EACH OTHER IN ALBANIA BY TOUCHING TEMPLES -SYMBOLIZING THAT THEIR THOUGHTS OF EACH OTHER ARE SINCERE

THE STRING-OF-BUTTONS CACTUS (Crassula perforata) ACTUALLY LOOKS LIKE BUTTONS STRUNG ON A THREAD

BILLY PHILLIPS of Nashville, Tenn., A LAD OF 16 WHO WAS DISPATCHED BY GEN. ANDREW JACKSON TO WARN AMERICANS THAT THE WAR OF 1812 HAD BEGUN, RODE 860 MILES ON HORSEBACK IN 9 DAYS -AVERAGING 95 MILES A DAY FOR 9 CONSECUTIVE DAYS

THE MOTHER WHOSE GREED KILLED HER OWN SON!
ISOBEL SINCLAIR, IN AN ATTEMPT TO MAKE HER SON HEIR TO THE SUTHERLAND FORTUNE, INVITED THE 10th EARL OF SUTHERLAND AND HIS WIFE AND SON TO A BANQUET AT HELMSDALE, Scotland, *AND SERVED POISONED ALE* — THE EARL AND HIS WIFE DIED, BUT THEIR SON ESCAPED UNHARMED—AND IN THE EXCITEMENT *ISOBEL'S OWN SON DRANK THE POISONED BEVERAGE AND DIED*

HINDENBURG'S FACE
Dickenson County, Va.;
NATURAL STONE FORMATION

THE LLANFRYNACH CHURCH
in Penllyne, Wales, WHICH IS PARTIALLY IN RUINS, STILL *HOLDS SERVICES ONCE A YEAR*

THOUSANDS OF TEMPLES
in India
ARE DEDICATED TO 2
MEMBERS OF THE HINDU
TRINITY, VISHNU AND SIVA-
YET BRAHMA, THE LEADING
FIGURE IN THE HINDU
TRINITY, HAS ONLY
A SINGLE TEMPLE
IT IS LOCATED ON THE
SHORE OF LAKE PUSHKAR,
NEAR Ajmere

BEDOUIN WOMEN
of Jebel Druse, Syria,
BY SMOKING LONG
CHURCH-WARDEN PIPES
PROCLAIM THAT THEY ARE MARRIED

HUMMINGBIRDS
NORMALLY
WARM-BLOODED
REVERT TO THEIR
REPTILE ANCESTRY
WHEN THE
TEMPERATURE DROPS
*- AND BECOME
COLD-BLOODED
CREATURES*

THE MELANESIAN COLLEGE
in Auckland N.Z.,
WAS BUILT IN 1858 - *WITH THE PROCEEDS
OF A SINGLE BOOK* - "The Daisy Chain"

THE GREATEST TREASURE IN THE SEAS

THE "ADMIRAL NAKHIMOV" an armored Russian cruiser TORPEDOED BY THE JAPANESE IN THE BATTLE OF TSUSHIMA IN 1905 HAS NEVER BEEN SALVAGED ALTHOUGH *IT CARRIED $92,750,000 IN GOLD SOVEREIGNS* IT LIES AT A DEPTH OF 300 FEET AND THE SEAS OVER IT ARE ALWAYS TURBULENT

THE TUNA

IS THE ONLY WARM-BLOODED FISH ITS DIGESTIVE SYSTEM IS SO UNDER-SIZED IN PROPORTION TO ITS BODY THAT TO SECURE THE ENERGY NECESSARY FOR SWIMMING FAST IT HAD TO BE PROVIDED BY NATURE WITH *GREATER HEAT TO SPEED UP ITS DIGESTIVE PROCESS*

HAPLOPHRYNE DEEP SEA ANGLERS FOUND IN THE ATLANTIC AT A DEPTH OF 1,000 FEET ARE ENCASED IN A JELLY-LIKE SUBSTANCE WHICH REDUCES THEIR SPECIFIC GRAVITY AND INCREASES THEIR ABILITY TO FLOAT

KING CHARLES I of England A LIFELONG STAMMERER UTTERED ONLY ONE SENTENCE WITHOUT STUTTERING- *HIS FARE-WELL MESSAGE ON JAN.30,1649 JUST BEFORE AN EXECUTIONER CHOPPED OFF HIS HEAD*

SHOES 2 FEET LONG WERE WORN BY KING PHILIP IV OF FRANCE -WHO MADE IT A CRIME FOR ANY SUBJECT TO OWN FOOTWEAR LONGER THAN HIS

THE CITY HALL of Pula, Yugoslavia, WAS BUILT INSIDE AN ANCIENT ROMAN TEMPLE CONSTRUCTED NEARLY 2,000 YEARS EARLIER

DUKE EMMANUEL PHILIBERT (1528-1580) of Savoia, Italy, BECAME A CARDINAL AT THE AGE OF 4

GEORGE WASHINGTON
Mohonk, N.Y.
NATURAL STONE FORMATION

SHEEP WHICH TRIMMED THE WHITE HOUSE LAWNS DURING WOODROW WILSON'S PRESIDENCY CONTRIBUTED TO THE RED CROSS 96 POUNDS OF WOOL -SOLD AT AUCTION FOR $100,000

THE **PISTOLAXE** A 16TH-CENTURY WEAPON THAT WAS BOTH A PISTOL AND A BATTLE AXE

THE **LEMON VINE** (Pereskia aculeata) WHICH STILL FLOURISHES IN the West Indies IS THE PARENT PLANT FROM WHICH ALL CACTI EVOLVED 60,000,000 YEARS AGO

A **HAT** THAT LOOKS LIKE A BOWL OF FRUIT IS WORN BY WOMEN of the Gutach Valley, Germany, TO INDICATE THEIR MARITAL STATUS IF THE KNITTED POMPONS ARE RED THE WEARER IS SINGLE BUT IF THEY ARE BLACK SHE ALREADY HAS A HUSBAND

THE
BAPTISMAL FONT
of the Church of Cadenet,
France,
*WAS MADE FROM A 2,000-
YEAR-OLD ROMAN BATHTUB*

DORA LILLIAN FLINN
TAUGHT SCHOOL
in Fort Ritner,
Indiana, in 1898
*ALTHOUGH SHE WAS
A DEAF MUTE*

THE STONE FISH
(Synancea verrucosa)
*LOOKS LIKE A
MOSS-COVERED ROCK—
A PERSON STEPPING ON IT
WITH LIGHTLY SHOD
FEET WILL SUFFER
EXCRUCIATING PAIN,*

THE ROOSTER'S HEAD
in the Matterhorn Region of Switzerland
NATURAL ROCK FORMATION

THE SLEEVE TOMB in Kamakura, Japan, HAS LONG BEEN A PLACE OF SACRED PILGRIMAGE —YET IT CONTAINS ONLY THE SLEEVE OF THE ROBE OF A CHILD WHO PERISHED WITH OTHER MEMBERS OF HIS FAMILY IN A FIRE 763 YEARS AGO

SULTAN MEDANGBA Chief of the Ituri dwarfs of Africa WEARS AN ANTELOPE TAIL AS HIS CEREMONIAL GARB AND HIS THRONE IS A STOOL SET UP IN A STRAW BASKET WHICH TRAVELS WITH HIM WHEREVER HE GOES

THE **COTTON SPINNER** PROTECTS ITSELF BY SPINNING A NET OF STICKY THREADS WHICH HARDENS IN THE WATER AND ENTRAPS THE ATTACKING FISH OR CRABS

THE **BRAZILIAN CATFROG** CLIMBS A TREE THAT EXTENDS OVER WATER AND FORMS A LEAF INTO THE SHAPE OF A CONE —IN WHICH THE FEMALE LAYS HER EGGS WHEN THE YOUNG EMERGE FROM THE EGGS THEY FALL DIRECTLY INTO THE WATER

THE SCRUB TURKEY of Australia IS HATCHED FULLY FEATHERED —AND FLIES AWAY FROM ITS NEST IMMEDIATELY

NICOLAS BAILLOT (1791-1896)
A NAPOLEONIC SOLDIER CAPTURED IN THE BATTLE OF WATERLOO, WAS FREED IN 1815 ON A DOCTOR'S VERDICT THAT HE WAS NEAR DEATH FROM TUBERCULOSIS – YET HE SURVIVED FOR 81 YEARS

DAVID RAMSEY (1749-1815)
AMERICAN HISTORIAN, LEGISLATOR AND PHYSICIAN, WAS AN ACADEMIC TUTOR *AT THE AGE OF 12*

HE WAS KILLED WHILE CONDUCTING A LEGAL EXAMINATION OF A DEFENDANT—WHO FIRED 3 SHOTS INTO THE DOCTOR *TO PROVE HE WAS INSANE*

THE LARGEST WOODEN CHURCH IN GERMANY
THE CHURCH OF THE HOLY GHOST in Clausthal-Zellerfeld, Germany, SEATS 2,200 PERSONS AND IS CONSTRUCTED ENTIRELY OF WOOD

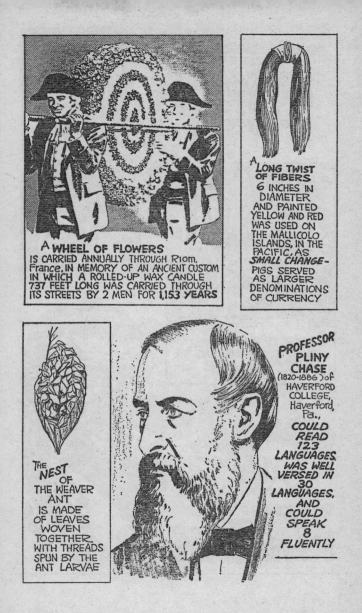

A **WHEEL OF FLOWERS** IS CARRIED ANNUALLY THROUGH Riom, France, IN MEMORY OF AN ANCIENT CUSTOM IN WHICH A ROLLED-UP WAX CANDLE 737 FEET LONG WAS CARRIED THROUGH ITS STREETS BY 2 MEN FOR 1,153 YEARS

A **LONG TWIST OF FIBERS** 6 INCHES IN DIAMETER AND PAINTED YELLOW AND RED WAS USED ON THE MALLICOLO ISLANDS, IN THE PACIFIC, AS *SMALL CHANGE*— PIGS SERVED AS LARGER DENOMINATIONS OF CURRENCY

THE **NEST** OF THE WEAVER ANT IS MADE OF LEAVES WOVEN TOGETHER WITH THREADS SPUN BY THE ANT LARVAE

PROFESSOR **PLINY CHASE** (1820-1886) of HAVERFORD COLLEGE, Haverford, Pa., *COULD READ 123 LANGUAGES, WAS WELL VERSED IN 30 LANGUAGES, AND COULD SPEAK 8 FLUENTLY*

GENERAL BEAUMONT de CARRIERE INFORMED THAT HE HAD BEEN MADE A MEMBER OF THE FRENCH GENERAL STAFF WAS SO OVERCOME WITH EMOTION THAT *HE DROPPED DEAD* 1813

THE **TOWER OF ULM**, Germany, WHICH HAS BEEN STANDING SINCE 1578 *LEANS 4 FEET, 8 INCHES OFF CENTER*

THE **OFFICIATING LAMA** at a Tibetan funeral IN WHICH THE CORPSE IS ALWAYS LEFT EXPOSED ON A MOUNTAIN, BLOWS A TRUMPET MADE FROM A HUMAN THIGHBONE *TO SUMMON THE HOVERING VULTURES*

THE LITTLE CORELLA AN AUSTRALIAN COCKATOO (Ducorpsius sanguineus) DINES WITHOUT HARM ON THE SEEDS OF THE PADDYMELON —YET THE SAME SEEDS WILL BLIND AND PARALYZE A HORSE

FRANCESCO AVELLONI (1756-1837) THE ITALIAN PLAYWRIGHT WROTE 600 PLAYS 32 OF HIS 5-ACT PLAYS EACH WERE WRITTEN BETWEEN DUSK AND DAWN OF A SINGLE NIGHT

THE CATHEDRAL OF ULM in Germany WHICH HAS THE TALLEST SPIRE IN THE WORLD (528'2") WAS UNDER CONSTRUCTION FOR 513 YEARS (1377-1890)

THE RAINCOATS WORN BY NATIVES OF THE ALEUTIAN ISLANDS ARE MADE FROM THE INTESTINES OF SEALS

THE "OSTRICH WORM" THE LONG SIPHON WORM HIDES FROM ITS ENEMIES *BY TURNING ITS HEAD INSIDE ITS BODY*

THE **TOWN HALL** of Neufchâteau, Belgium, *HOUSES THE TOWN COUNCIL, THE JAIL AND THE SCHOOL*

THE **SHERPAS** famed Himalayan mountaineers CONSIDER A HUSBAND AND WIFE DIVORCED *WHEN THEY BREAK A STRING*

THE CHURCH of ST. JOHN THE BAPTIST in Campi Bisenzio, Italy, BEING AN OASIS OF REST FOR WEARY TRAVELERS, IS BUILT IN THE SHAPE OF A TENT

TITIAN (1477-1576) the celebrated painter DIED OF THE PLAGUE AND HIS BODY WAS SECRETLY INCINERATED- BUT HE WAS SO POPULAR THAT OFFICIALS ANNOUNCED HE HAD DIED A NATURAL DEATH AND STAGED A FAKE FUNERAL-USING A COFFIN CONTAINING A HEAVY ROCK

THE HUGE ORNAMENTAL CROWN SURMOUNTING EACH PAIR OF COLUMNS IN THE MONASTERY OF SILOS, SPAIN, WAS CARVED FROM A SINGLE BLOCK OF MARBLE

THE CATHEDRAL of ST. FLOUR
France
FOR 400 YEARS PERMITTED USE OF ONE OF ITS TOWERS AS A PRISON AND THE OTHER AS THE SCENE FOR AN *ANNUAL BANQUET HONORING THE TOWN'S SHOEMAKERS*

SIR WINSTON CHURCHILL
(1874-1965)
WHOSE FATHER DIED ON JAN. 24, 1895, HAD EXPRESSED A WISH TO DIE ON THE ANNIVERSARY OF HIS FATHER'S DEMISE
SIR WINSTON DIED ON THE 70TH ANNIVERSARY OF HIS FATHER'S DEATH- WITHIN 90 MINUTES OF THE EXACT HOUR

THE VERTICAL FISH
A TYPE OF FISH THAT SWIMS ALMOST UPRIGHT AT A DEPTH OF 2,500 FEET, WAS SIGHTED BY EXPLORER CHARLES BEEBE FROM HIS BATHYSPHERE-YET *THIS KIND OF FISH HAS NEVER BEEN SEEN AGAIN*

THE FROZEN WATERFALL of Mt. Beardmore, in the Antarctic HAS A HEIGHT OF MORE THAN 10,000 FEET *- 60 TIMES THAT OF NIAGARA FALLS*

A **LIGHT PLANE**
FLOWN BY AYLIFFE CAREY,
MAGISTRATE OF STEWART, BRITISH COLUMBIA,
FLEW HEAD-ON INTO A PRECIPICE IN A
SNOWSTORM-YET CAREY WHEN HE
WAS RESCUED THE NEXT DAY BY
HELICOPTER *HAD NOT SUFFERED*
A SINGLE BROKEN BONE
HIS PLANE HAD WEDGED ITSELF INTO
A ROCKY CREVICE WITH ITS TAIL
HANGING OVER A 2,000-FOOT CLIFF
AND THE DRUMS OF GASOLINE IT
CARRIED AS CARGO STILL INTACT
October 14, 1968

THE **MALE FLATHEAD FISH** of Brazil CARRIES THE EGGS OF ITS YOUNG- UNTIL THEY HATCH

AVICENNA (980-1037) ARABIAN
"Prince of Physicians"
MEMORIZED A LIBRARY OF **50**
GREEK BOOKS ON PHILOSOPHY AND
MATH AT THE AGE OF 14, ABSORBED
THE CONTENTS OF **70** BOOKS ON
MEDICINE AND BECAME A PHYSICIAN
AT 16 AND 2 YEARS LATER HAD
MEMORIZED SEVERAL HUNDRED
VOLUMES ON SCIENCE,
MATH AND MEDICINE

KING SELEUCUS
(358-281 B.C.) of Syria
FOUNDED 32 CITIES
-EACH OF WHICH BECAME A
CENTER OF GREEK CULTURE
HE NAMED 16 OF THE CITIES
AFTER HIS FATHER, ANTIOCH

THE MEMORIAL TOWER
of Mohonk, N.Y.,
MARKS THE BORDER OF
3 TOWNSHIPS AND
OVERLOOKS 6 STATES
N.Y., CONN., MASS.,
VT., N.J. AND PA.

ANNE BRADSTREET (1613-1672)
DAUGHTER OF GOVERNOR THOMAS
DUDLEY AND WIFE OF GOVERNOR
SIMON BRADSTREET OF COLONIAL
MASSACHUSETTS, WAS THE
FIRST AMERICAN POETESS

ALTHOUGH IN DUST
I NOW DO LIE
REMEMBER YOU
MUST SHORTLY BE
LAID IN THE DUST
TO SLEEP WITH ME

EPITAPH IN OLD SOUTH
SALEM CEMETERY, N.Y.

DESERT ANTS in Atacama, Chile, TO REACH UNDERGROUND STREAMS DIG PASSAGES THAT DESCEND MANY YARDS BELOW THE SURFACE OF THE DESERT

A **FROG** (*Rana Fasciata*) in South Africa MADE A LEAP OF *14 FEET*

BARNET BURNS an English sailor WHO WAS MADE CHIEF OF A TRIBE OF 600 MAORI NATIVES IN N. ZEALAND, WAS FIRST REQUIRED TO SUBMIT TO *TATTOOING OVER EVERY INCH OF HIS BODY FROM HEAD TO FOOT*— HIS REIGN STARTED IN 1832 AND LASTED ONLY TWO YEARS

"BILLY" A HOMING PIGEON OWNED BY HUGH PERKINS, of Summersville, W.Va., APPEARED AT THE WINDOW OF THE BOY'S HOSPITAL ROOM IN PHILIPPI 10 DAYS AFTER THE OWNER HAD LEFT HOME—*HAVING TRAVELED 105 MILES AND LOCATED THE PROPER WINDOW LEDGE A BAND ON THE PIGEON'S LEG WAS POSITIVE IDENTIFICATION (1939)*

THE STATUE THAT AGED

THE STONE LIKENESS OF EMPEROR RUDOLPH I of Germany (1218-1291) WHICH STANDS ON HIS GRAVE IN THE CATHEDRAL OF SPEYER WAS CARVED IN 1281 BY A SCULPTOR WHO FOLLOWED THE RULER ABOUT FOR YEARS —SO HE COULD ACHIEVE A TRUE DEPICTION *BY ADDING EACH NEW WRINKLE AS THE MONARCH AGED*

THE HUTS of the Ragyabas of Lhasa, Tibet, ADVERTISE THEIR OCCUPATION AS SCAVENGERS— HAVING INSERTED IN THE MORTAR *HORNS FROM CATTLE THAT DIED IN THE AREA*

T. WISTER BROWN SERVED ON THE BOARD OF MANAGERS OF HAVERFORD COLLEGE, HAVERFORD, PA. FROM 1853 TO 1916 —A PERIOD OF 63 YEARS

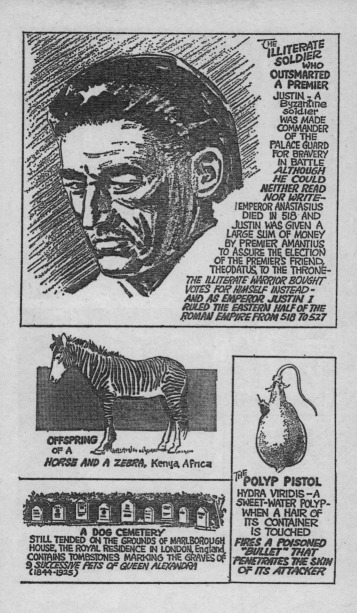

THE ILLITERATE SOLDIER WHO OUTSMARTED A PREMIER

JUSTIN - A Byzantine soldier WAS MADE COMMANDER OF THE PALACE GUARD FOR BRAVERY IN BATTLE *ALTHOUGH HE COULD NEITHER READ NOR WRITE* - ! EMPEROR ANASTASIUS DIED IN 518 AND JUSTIN WAS GIVEN A LARGE SUM OF MONEY BY PREMIER AMANTIUS TO ASSURE THE ELECTION OF THE PREMIER'S FRIEND, THEODATUS, TO THE THRONE - *THE ILLITERATE WARRIOR BOUGHT VOTES FOR HIMSELF INSTEAD - AND AS EMPEROR JUSTIN I RULED THE EASTERN HALF OF THE ROMAN EMPIRE FROM 518 To 527*

OFFSPRING OF A HORSE AND A ZEBRA, Kenya, Africa

THE POLYP PISTOL

HYDRA VIRIDIS — A SWEET-WATER POLYP— WHEN A HAIR OF ITS CONTAINER IS TOUCHED *FIRES A POISONED "BULLET" THAT PENETRATES THE SKIN OF ITS ATTACKER*

A DOG CEMETERY STILL TENDED ON THE GROUNDS OF MARLBOROUGH HOUSE, THE ROYAL RESIDENCE IN LONDON, England, CONTAINS TOMBSTONES MARKING THE GRAVES OF 9 SUCCESSIVE PETS OF QUEEN ALEXANDRA (1844-1925)

THE **4** COLUMNS SUPPORTING THE ROOF OF THE STAIRWAY OF THE TOWN HALL OF Duderstadt, Germany, WERE EACH CARVED IN 1673 FROM *THE TRUNK OF A SINGLE OAK TREE*

DINNIE MYERS an Australian aborigine WAS THE LAST SURVIVING MEMBER OF THE MILDURA TRIBE

SHEEP in Tibet ARE USED AS *BEASTS OF BURDEN* THEY CARRY 30-LB. LOADS OF GRAIN AND FLOUR

THE **GREAT BUDDHA** in the Lamasery of Tashi Lhunpo, in Communist Tibet, HAS BEEN WIRED FOR ELECTRICITY *AND NOW HAS A LIGHT BULB IN ITS GOLDEN CROWN*

ELM TREE in St. Joseph, Mo., 2 FEET IN DIAMETER *FELLED BY C.G. WILSON WITH .22-CALIBER BULLETS*

THE EXECUTIONER OF CHARLOTTE CORDAY WAS SO INCENSED AT THE GIRL'S CRIME OF HAVING MURDERED MARAT, THAT AFTER THE GUILLOTINE'S BLADE FELL, HE HELD UP HER HEAD BY ITS LONG HAIR AND SLAPPED HER FACE! *INSTANTLY, THE FACE, WHICH HAD BEEN A DEATHLY WHITE FLUSHED DEEP RED* (July 17, 1793)

PAULINE SISTER OF NAPOLEON BONAPARTE WORE GOWNS MADE OF MUSLIN SO THIN *THE MATERIAL HAD TO BE WOVEN UNDER WATER TO PREVENT THE THREADS FROM BREAKING*

SEEDS OF THE MANGROVE TREE GERMINATE WHILE STILL ATTACHED TO THE TREE

THE PHANTOM SHIP
A NATURAL ROCK FORMATION in Crater Lake, Oregon, THAT APPEARS TO BE A *FULL-RIGGED SHIP AND ITS CREW*

AN OPTICAL ILLUSION, IT VANISHES FROM TIME TO TIME BY BLENDING WITH THE CLIFF BEHIND IT, THEN SUDDENLY REAPPEARS

BARON ANTON ULRICH von HOLZHAUSEN (1754-1832)
WAS THE 36th MEMBER OF HIS FAMILY TO SERVE AS MAYOR OF FRANKFURT ON THE MAIN, GERMANY

THE TOWER of La BATIAZ
in Martigny, France, BUILT IN THE 13TH CENTURY IS EXACTLY 114 FEET HIGH AND 114 FEET IN CIRCUMFERENCE

GEORGIAN BAY
(an arm of Lake Huron)
THAT IS 5800 SQUARE
MILES IN SIZE
*CONTAINS 30,000
ISLANDS* (canada)

JACQUES DAUDÉ
PURCHASED FOR HIMSELF AND HIS
SUCCESSORS THE PERPETUAL OFFICE
OF MAYOR OF LE VIGAN, FRANCE, IN 1693
FOR $2,373 - JACQUES, HIS SON AND
GRANDSON FILLED THE POST SUCCESSIVELY
UNTIL 1774 - *WHEN THE CITY ENDED ITS CONTRACT
BY REFUNDING THE ORIGINAL PAYMENT*

A GRAVE
UNEARTHED IN Helmsdorf, Germany,
*SHAPED EXACTLY LIKE A
PREHISTORIC HUMAN DWELLING*

PETREL
a small sea bird
DRINKS ONLY
SEA WATER
AND IF LEFT INLAND
BESIDE FRESH WATER
WILL DIE OF THIRST

THE PROPHET OF DOOM

LORENZO MANCINI
the Italian astrologer,
ACCURATELY PREDICTED
HIS OWN DEATH AND THE
DAY ON WHICH HIS SON
PAOLO WOULD DIE IN
1652 -- *AND PROPHESIED
HIS WIFE WOULD DIE IN
THE YEAR 1656* --

HIS WIDOW, SISTER OF
CARDINAL MAZARIN,
DIED SUDDENLY ON
DEC. 29, 1656

DOORS AND WINDOWS
in Kafiristan, Asia,
ARE CONSTRUCTED IN A
LATTICE PATTERN - *COPIED
FROM THE SUNGLASSES
WITH WOODEN LATTICEWORK
WORN BY NATIVES*

A FOUR-WHEELER
PEDALLED BY A FOOTMAN, WAS
DEMONSTRATED IN PARIS, FRANCE, IN
1779 - *61 YEARS BEFORE THE
INVENTION OF THE BICYCLE*

"39" ISLAND - Zante, Greece
ITS NAME IS A REMINDER THAT
IN 1808 *39 NOBLES WERE
EXECUTED HERE*

ROPE MAKERS in Kiangsi, China, WORK IN WOODEN TOWERS 30 FEET HIGH *IN THE BELIEF THAT ROPES PLAITED VERTICALLY ARE STRONGER THAN THOSE MADE HORIZONTALLY*

THE MAN WHOSE LIFE WAS SAVED BY LOVE

THE 5TH EARL OF BALCARRES in Scotland REJECTED BY THE GIRL HE LOVED, WAS ON HIS DEATH-BED WHEN SHE LEARNED HE HAD GENEROUSLY BEQUEATHED HER HALF HIS FORTUNE—

THE GIRL RUSHED TO THE DYING EARL WITH A PROMISE TO RECONSIDER— *AFTER WHICH HE QUICKLY RECOVERED AND THEY WERE HAPPILY MARRIED FOR 18 YEARS*

THE BLADDERWORT an aquatic plant that floats in ponds, HAS TRAP DOORS IN ITS LEAVES THROUGH WHICH MINUTE WATER ORGANISMS ENTER —*BUT CAN NEVER LEAVE*— THE DEAD BODIES OF THE ORGANISMS HELP KEEP THE PLANT AFLOAT

ANN NESBIT
WORKED AS A GOVERNESS FOR THE WILLIAM ROBINSON FAMILY OF CHEVIOT, N.Z. *FOR 70 YEARS*

THE **ROAD THAT WAS BUILT BY A METEOR**
KING LOUIS XIV of France ORDERED A MILITARY HIGHWAY CONSTRUCTED THROUGH GREAT BAYARD ROCK, near Dinant, Belgium, AND ON THE EVE OF THE DAY WORK WAS TO HAVE BEEN STARTED - A *FALLING METEOR SPLIT THE ROCK TO CREATE A NATURAL ROADWAY* THE HIGHWAY THUS FORMED ON MAY 29, 1698, IS STILL IN USE 270 YEARS LATER

THE **MAP** of New Brunswick CANADA'S "PICTURE PROVINCE" WHEN VIEWED UPSIDE DOWN FORMS A LIKENESS OF JACQUES CARTIER ‑DISCOVERER OF THE ST. LAWRENCE RIVER

NEW BRUNSWICK

THE SURGEON FISH IS ARMED WITH 2 "SCALPELS" ‑ONE ON EITHER SIDE NEAR ITS TAIL‑ WHICH IT CAN SWING OUT FROM ITS BODY TO SLASH AT ANY ENEMY

THE **TWIN PEN PAGODAS** in Soochow, China, AND A COMPANION "INK PAGODA" WERE BUILT 1,000 YEARS AGO BY A FATHER TO MAKE SURE *HIS SON WAS SUCCESSFUL IN A SCHOOL EXAMINATION*

KING ORODES I of Parthia WHO ABDICATED HIS THRONE IN 37 B.C. IN FAVOR OF HIS BELOVED SON, PHRAATES, *WAS MURDERED BY THE NEW MONARCH AS HIS FIRST OFFICIAL ACT—* PHRAATES ALSO KILLED 29 OF HIS BROTHERS

THE **CHURCH OF ST. LÉRY** in France HAS IN ITS BELFRY A CLOCK WITH NO DIAL *THE CLOCK RINGS OUT THE HOURS*

DRUMS on the island of Timor, in Malaya, ARE CARVED IN THE SHAPE OF A HUMAN TORSO *BECAUSE AN ANCIENT TRIBAL HERO COULD IMITATE THE SOUND OF A DRUM BY THUMPING ON HIS CHEST*

SOMEBODY'S
DARLING LIES
BURIED HERE
1865 ERECTED 1903

Epitaph ON THE
TOMBSTONE OF AN
UNKNOWN MAN
near the Molyneux River, N.Z.

GENKU (1133-1212.)
Japanese
religious leader,
DEVOTING ALL HIS
WAKING MOMENTS
TO PRAYER,
PRONOUNCED THE JAPANESE
NAME FOR "BUDDHA"
60,000 TIMES EACH
DAY FOR 30 YEARS

LIVING CALENDARS
GIRLS on the island of Helgoland
CELEBRATED NEW YEAR'S DAY IN 1866 BY
WEARING DRESSES ON WHICH WAS PRINTED
THE ENTIRE CALENDAR OF THE YEAR

"ME AND MY SHADOW"
THE INK SQUID
FOOLS PURSUERS BY DISCHARGING
A BLACK FLUID THAT FORMS
THE SAME SHAPE AS THE SQUID

THE **LIVING FEATHER DUSTERS**
CASUARINA TREES of Australia
HAVE FOLIAGE
RESEMBLING FEATHERS

AGLAIS of Athens
a famed lady trumpet player
DAILY ATE 12 POUNDS OF MEAT
AND 8 POUNDS OF BREAD—*AND*
WASHED DOWN HER DINNER
WITH 3 QUARTS OF WINE

LOCH MAREE
in New Zealand
STILL IS DOTTED WITH
THE TRUNKS OF TREES
INUNDATED WHEN
A LANDSLIDE
DAMMED THE
SEAFORTH RIVER
UNKNOWN
CENTURIES
AGO

THE **PAUL SAUER BRIDGE**
over the Storm River Gorge, South Africa,
WHICH SPANS A CHASM 400 FEET DEEP
IS SUPPORTED BY 2 HUGE GIRDERS
WHICH WERE SUNK VERTICALLY
INTO THE ROCK—AND THEN
BENT INTO AN ARCH—JOINING
PERFECTLY AT THE CENTER

RENÉ-AUGUSTE de **RENNEVILLE**
(1650 - 1723)
A PRISONER IN THE BASTILLE FOR 11 YEARS,
AND DENIED USE OF PEN OR PENCIL,
WROTE 6,000 LINES OF ROMANTIC
POETRY AND A HISTORY OF 10 VOLUMES
-USING SPLIT CHICKEN BONES, DIPPED
IN A MIXTURE OF SOOT AND WINE

STONE CLOWN
Nankendorf, Germany,
NATURAL ROCK FORMATION

THE **TOWN** THAT **NEVER SEES THE WINTER SUN** RJUKAN A COMMUNITY OF 6,000 PERSONS in Norway IS SURROUNDED BY MOUNTAINS SO HIGH THAT THROUGHOUT THE WINTER ITS INHABITANTS *NEVER SEE THE SUN*

MARGARET FINCH (1631-1740) a gypsy queen in Kent, England, SAT SO LONG WITH HER KNEES BENT BENEATH HER THAT FOR THE FINAL 40 YEARS OF HER LIFE *SHE WAS UNABLE TO STAND ON HER FEET* SHE WAS BURIED AT THE AGE OF 109 IN A SQUARE COFFIN -WITH HER KNEES STILL BENT

"LEENA" a french poodle *WITH 3 TOES ON EACH FRONT FOOT*

A ROWBOAT PRESENTED TO CZAR IVAN THE TERRIBLE BY QUEEN ELIZABETH I OF ENGLAND IS CALLED "THE GRANDFATHER OF THE RUSSIAN NAVY" - CZAR PETER THE GREAT, IN 1688, *MADE IT THE FIRST VESSEL OF A POWERFUL NAVY HE ASSEMBLED*

EMPEROR ALEXIUS III (1170-1210) of Byzance SUFFERED SO MUCH PAIN FROM GOUT THAT HIS REGULAR MEANS OF FINDING RELIEF WAS APPLYING A *RED-HOT POKER TO HIS FEET*

KNOTTED STRINGS USED FOR BOOKKEEPING RECORDS BY THE ANCIENT PERUVIANS, WERE COUNTED IN UNITS OF 10, IN THE DECIMAL SYSTEM -ALTHOUGH AMERICAN INDIANS OF THAT PERIOD ALWAYS COUNTED BY 20's

MARTIN BORMANN HITLER'S CLOSEST CONFIDANT WHO VANISHED AFTER THE COLLAPSE OF THE THIRD REICH ALWAYS WORE 3 SIGNET RINGS -EACH FILLED WITH POISON

A **WHALEBOAT**
ON THE BARK "CICERO"
out of Falmouth, Mass.,
*WAS CHEWED UP
AND SWALLOWED
BY A WHALE*

THE CREW ESCAPED
AND WAS RESCUED BY
OTHER FISHERMEN
Jan. 14, 1864

The
"**HIPPIE**"
CRAB
Pilumnus
novaezelandiae
IT IS COVERED
WITH A BUSHY
GROWTH OF HAIR

**NICCOLO GIOSAFATTE
BIAGIOLI** (1768-1830)

WAS A PROFESSOR OF
GREEK AND LATIN
AT THE UNIVERSITY OF ROME, ITALY,
AT THE AGE OF 16

THE SLEEPING MOUNTAIN of MOROCCO
JEBEL MUSA, near Tetuan,
FORMS THE OUTLINE OF A
SLUMBERING GIANT

Dr. PIERRE CHARMEIL
(1782-1830) A FRENCH SURGEON
WAS IN CHARGE OF AMPUTATIONS IN THE
MILITARY HOSPITAL IN METZ, FRANCE,
WHEN HE WAS ONLY 16 YEARS OF AGE

THE EARTH STAR
a puffball fungus
GETS ITS NAME
FROM THE FACT
THAT ITS OUTER
SKIN SPLITS
INTO PIECES
THAT FORM A STAR

THE GUM TREES
of Australia
HOLD THEIR LEAVES ALL
YEAR BUT ANNUALLY
SHED THEIR BARK

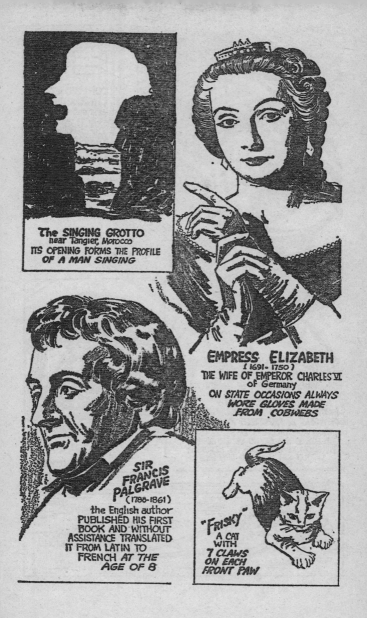

The SINGING GROTTO
near Tangier, Morocco
ITS OPENING FORMS THE PROFILE
OF A MAN SINGING

EMPRESS ELIZABETH
(1691 - 1750)
THE WIFE OF EMPEROR CHARLES VI
of Germany
ON STATE OCCASIONS ALWAYS
WORE GLOVES MADE
FROM COBWEBS

SIR
FRANCIS
PALGRAVE
(1788-1861)
the English author
PUBLISHED HIS FIRST
BOOK AND WITHOUT
ASSISTANCE TRANSLATED
IT FROM LATIN TO
FRENCH AT THE
AGE OF 8

"FRISKY"
A CAT
WITH
7 CLAWS
ON EACH
FRONT PAW

A CUNEIFORM CHARACTER from ancient Babylon WHICH HAS 5 DIFFERENT MEANINGS AND MAY BE PRONOUNCED AS "LAL" "LIB" "LUB" "PAH" OR "NAR"

THE AUTHOR WHO NEVER WASTED A SHEET OF PAPER

ABUL ALA ZOHR of Seville AUTHORED 50 BOOKS ON MEDICINE AND BOTANY -WRITING EACH ON THE NARROW MARGINS OF PAGES IN PREVIOUSLY PUBLISHED BOOKS

KING ALMOTADDHED OF SEVILLE APPOINTED HIM GRAND VIZIER OF HIS KINGDOM IN THE BELIEF HIS FRUGALITY WOULD SET A GOOD EXAMPLE

A CURTAIN in the Church of ALL SAINTS, in Sedlec, Czechoslovakia, THE ELABORATE FOLDS OF WHICH ARE MADE OF MATCHED HUMAN BONES

THE STALK-EYED SQUID HAS ITS EYES AT THE END OF 2 HORN-LIKE EXTENSIONS

LIGHTNING FORMING A PROFILE OF NIKITA KHRUSHCHEV
Photographed by GEORGE DAVIS
Downers Grove, Ill.

THE CEREMONIAL DRUMS
USED BY THE LAMBAS of Zambia, Africa, ARE MADE IN THE SHAPE OF *DUGOUT CANOES*

THE **FIRST ARTIFICIAL LIMB**
AN IRON HAND ORDERED BY KING ROBERT the BRUCE of Scotland
FOR A KNIGHT NAMED De.CLEPHANES
MORE THAN 650 YEARS AGO
EACH FINGER COULD BE MOVED BY PRESSING A BUTTON

THE **RULER** WHO GAVE EVERY ROBBER LICENSE TO LOOT AND KILL!
GARCIA de AVELLANEDA
Spanish Viceroy of Naples
FACING AN ENEMY INVASION IN 1654 WITHOUT MEANS OF DEFENSE APPEALED FOR AID TO THE COUNTRY'S NUMEROUS BANDS OF HIGHWAYMEN
THE BANDITS DEFEATED THE INVADING FRENCH ARMY – AND WERE GIVEN PERMISSION FOR THE VICEROY'S ENTIRE 7-YEAR REIGN *TO ROB AND MURDER WITHOUT FEAR OF PUNISHMENT!*

THE **FROG FISH** of Brazil CRAWLS ON DRY LAND -USING ITS FINS AS FEET IT CAN STAY OUT OF WATER AS LONG AS 3 DAYS

THE **GRAVESTONE** OF OSCAR AND MAGGIE DIETZEL, IN GREENWOOD CEMETERY, Brooklyn, N.Y., DEPICTS IN STARTLING DETAIL THE RAILROAD WRECK IN WHICH THEY WERE KILLED

HI. SIS!

'SIS' IN THE LANGUAGE OF ANCIENT CHALDEA MEANS "BROTHER"

NICHT ZU HAUSE

THE **DOOR** OF ADOLF MENZEL, the famed German painter, ALWAYS DISPLAYED A SIGN -NOT AT HOME- WHEN THE PAINTER WAS AT HOME- THE SIGN WAS REMOVED WHENEVER MENZEL WAS AWAY

LOUIS **PASTEUR** (1822-1895) MADE HIS IMMORTAL DISCOVERY THAT GERMS CAUSE DISEASE BECAUSE A MERCHANT ASKED HIM WHY A BATCH OF WINE HAD SOURED PASTEUR, PROFESSOR OF CHEMISTRY AT THE FACULTY OF SCIENCES, IN LILLE, FRANCE, STUDIED THE SUGAR BEET THROUGH A MICROSCOPE AND SAW THE TINY BODIES THAT CAUSED FERMENTATION, SPOILING- AND DISEASE (1854)

FARMHOUSES in Mehouneche, Algeria, AS PROTECTION AGAINST FLOODS AND BANDITS *ARE PERCHED ON VIRTUALLY INACCESSIBLE CLIFFS*

THE **MAN** WHO WAS HIS OWN GRANDNEPHEW RAYMOND VII (1197-1249) ruler of Toulouse, France, DISCARDED HIS FIRST WIFE TO MARRY MARGUERITE OF PROVENCE—*WHO WAS THE NIECE OF HIS NEPHEW*

THE **FIRST** CIGARS BROUGHT TO EUROPE BY SEAMEN IN THE 16th CENTURY CONSISTED OF CUT TOBACCO LEAVES INSIDE *CURVED CONES FORMED FROM PALM LEAVES*

ARCHBISHOP GASPARE RICCIULLI (1496-1592) OF REGGIO CALABRIA, ITALY, SERVED THE CHURCH FOR A PERIOD OF 71 YEARS

THE MAN WHO ORIGINATED NEWSPAPER ADVERTISING

DR. THEOPHRAST RENAUDOT (1586-1653) PUBLISHER OF THE GAZETTE DE FRANCE, IN PARIS, ADDED A SUPPLEMENT DEVOTED TO MERCHANDISE ADVERTISING IN 1633

LAWRENCE B. MASSEY of Carlisle, Pa., FISHING AT BROADKILL BEACH, DEL., HOOKED A SEA GULL AND A SHARK ON THE SAME CAST

THE CUSTOM OF DECORATING FOUNTAINS IN SPAIN WITH FLOWERS, STILL CARRIED OUT EACH OCT. 13th IN THE CATHEDRAL OF BARCELONA, WAS ORIGINATED BY THE ANCIENT IBERIANS 2,000 YEARS AGO

THE VEIL OF ICE
FRIGGA'S CAVE, in the Tennen Mountains of Salzburg, Austria, HAS AN ENTRANCE FRAMED BY A GIGANTIC CURTAIN OF ICE *-THE GRACEFUL FOLDS OF WHICH NEVER MELT*

BONAVENTURA van OVERBEEK (1660-1705) the celebrated Dutch painter HAD SUCH AN AVERSION TO STAIRWAYS THAT EACH HOME HE OCCUPIED COULD BE ENTERED ONLY BY *A LADDER WHICH HE WOULD PULL UP WHEN HE WANTED TO BE ALONE*

A WOMAN
of the Tumbuka Tribe, in Central Africa, WHO BECOMES THE MOTHER OF TWINS IS EXPELLED TO LIVE WITH HER HUSBAND IN THE FOREST *-EXISTING FOR 2 MONTHS WITHOUT SALT OR COOKED FOOD*

A CHILD'S SOCK
FOUND IN A GRAVE IN EGYPT, HAD BEEN KNITTED *1,500 YEARS AGO*

BARON de CHARNACÉ of France
HELD 3 MILITARY RANKS SIMULTANEOUSLY
HE WAS A COLONEL ON WEEKDAYS, A CAPTAIN EVERY SUNDAY, AND A FIELD MARSHAL ON EACH BIRTHDAY

THE HORSE THAT BROUGHT DEATH!
IT WAS CONSIDERED THE FINEST ANIMAL OF ITS TIME *BUT EVERY ONE OF ITS OWNERS MET A VIOLENT END!* SEIUS, THE ROMAN STATESMAN OF THE 1st CENTURY B.C. DIED BY TORTURE. GENERAL DOLABELLA, IN 43 B.C. ORDERED ONE OF HIS SOLDIERS TO KILL HIM. GAIUS CASSIUS, ITS NEXT OWNER, WAS EXECUTED. MARK ANTONY COMMITTED SUICIDE.
FOR CENTURIES ANY MAN PURSUED BY BAD FORTUNE WAS SAID TO "HAVE SEIUS' HORSE"

FARMERS in Burjasot, Spain, STILL STORE THEIR WHEAT IN UNDERGROUND PITS DUG BY THE ANCIENT ROMANS 1,900 YEARS AGO
EACH PIT IS SEALED BY A HUGE BOULDER-WHICH IS SECURED BY A HEAVY CHAIN AND PADLOCK

" PAVO'S TEDDY "
A HORSE OWNED BY MELVIN MARVIN of Eaton Rapids, Michigan,
HAS LEOPARD MARKINGS

A NEW GARDEN
started by Kaonde tribesmen of Africa
MUST BE MADE PRODUCTIVE BY
PLACING SOME FOOD BENEATH TWO
ANT HILLS WHICH ARE LEANED AGAINST
EACH OTHER TO FORM AN ARCH

MUSHROOM
GROWING OUT
OF ANOTHER
MUSHROOM

A CHICKEN
WITH 3 FEET

FARMERS
IN PARTS OF THE VALLEY OF NEPAL
MUST TURN THE SOIL BY HAND BECAUSE
IT IS FORBIDDEN BY LAW TO USE OXEN FOR PLOWING

THE FASCIST ARCH
in the Marmolada Glacier, Italy, WAS GIVEN THAT NAME BECAUSE IT APPEARED IN THE WINTER OF 1922, WHEN ITALY BECAME FASCIST, AND DISAPPEARED IN 1943 —THE YEAR IN WHICH THE FASCIST GOVERNMENT WAS DEPOSED

THE SOLDIER WHO HAD A CHARMED LIFE!
COUNT AUGUSTIN BELLIARD (1762-1832) A FRENCH GENERAL HAD 2 HORSES SHOT FROM UNDER HIM IN EACH OF 6 DIFFERENT BATTLES

MUSHROOMS PERSIST IN GROWING ON THE CARPET OF AN AUTOMOBILE OWNED BY MRS. TAK WOO, OF LOS ANGELES

PHILIPPE ANTOINE de CLARIS (1707-1767) WHOSE WIFE WAS A NIECE OF VOLTAIRE WAS THE FATHER OF 7 NUNS

EGGS
LAID BY
THE SOUTH
AFRICAN
LEOPARD
TORTOISE
LOOK
JUST LIKE
PING PONG
BALLS

**THE MAN WHO SET THE
DATE FOR CHRISTMAS**
Julius Sextus Africanus
a historian of Alexandria, Egypt,
IN HIS " CHRONICON FROM
THE CREATION OF THE
WORLD TO THE YEAR 221"
ESTABLISHED DECEMBER 25th AS
THE DATE OF THE NATIVITY

"BIG BEN"
A CROSS-BRED HEREFORD STEER —WEIGHED 4,700 POUNDS AND
MEASURED 16 FEET, 8 INCHES FROM ITS NOSE TO THE TIP OF ITS TAIL.

A MUSKET carried in the Battle of Gettysburg *RECEIVED A DIRECT HIT BY A CANNONBALL* THE BARREL WAS SPLINTERED AND EVERY SCREW IN THE WEAPON WAS LOOSENED -YET THE SOLDIER BEARING THE GUN DID *NOT DROP IT AND ESCAPED WITHOUT INJURY*

DANIS TRIBESMEN of New Guinea TO MOURN A RELATIVE OR REPENT A MISDEED *AMPUTATE ONE OF THEIR FINGERS*

THE *MUKISHI* A STICK CARRIED AS PROTECTION BY CHILDREN of the Kaonde Tribe of Africa, IS BELIEVED TO HOLD *THE SOUL OF A DEPARTED ANCESTOR*

WILLIAM COMBE (1741-1823) English author of 86 books and 200 biographies AFTER LOSING HIS FORTUNE HAD SERVED AS A SOLDIER, COOK AND WAITER, YET HE WAS SO HUMILIATED AT FINDING IT NECESSARY TO WRITE FOR A LIVING *THAT HE NEVER PERMITTED PUBLISHERS TO USE HIS NAME*

A PARRAKEET IS CALLED A "BUDGERIGAR" IN THE LANGUAGE OF THE AUSTRALIAN ABORIGINES BECAUSE THE WORD MEANS "GOOD FOOD"

THE MAN WHO WAS BURIED IN DUPLICATE!
GENERAL KUAN TI (162-219) of China
CAPTURED AND DECAPITATED WAS GIVEN 2 BURIALS WITH FULL MILITARY POMP

THE COMMANDING OFFICER OF HIS CAPTORS BURIED THE GENERAL'S HEAD ON A BODY CREATED OF SOLID GOLD - AND KUAN'S OWN FORCES BURIED HIS BODY WITH A HEAD SCULPTURED IN GOLD

FERTILE LAND IS SO VALUABLE IN TIRIOLO, ITALY, located on a mountain slope THAT VEGETABLES ARE PLANTED IN THE CRACKS OF STAIRWAYS LEADING TO EACH HOUSE

THE IRON BELL in Rocamadour, France, THAT HAS PEALED A WELCOME TO PILGRIMS FOR 1,200 YEARS, WAS HAMMERED OUT OF A SINGLE BLOCK OF FORGED IRON

JOACHIM PATINIER
(1475-1524)
a leading Flemish painter
WENT THROUGH HIS ENTIRE LIFE
WITHOUT EVER TAKING A BATH

DR. JAHIAL PARMLY
A DENTIST OF
Perry, Ohio,
WAS THE BROTHER OF
3 DENTISTS AND THE
UNCLE, BROTHER-IN-LAW
AND COUSIN OF
14 DENTISTS

THE
NASSAU GROUPER
CAN CAMOUFLAGE
ITSELF BY **8**
DIFFERENT COLOR
COMBINATIONS

GARY DOUGLAS GIBBS
of Bossier City, La.,
WHO WAS BORN WITH A HOLE IN THE WALL OF
HIS HEART, HAS A BIRTHMARK ON HIS BACK
— *DIRECTLY BEHIND HIS HEART* —
IN THE SHAPE OF A HEART

THE LARGEST ELEPHANT IN THE WORLD

A PHANTOM ELEPHANT THAT ROAMED THE MATTHEW RANGE OF THE NORTHERN GAME PRESERVE OF KENYA, AFRICA, FOR 75 YEARS, WAS PHOTOGRAPHED—YET NO ONE EVER SUCCEEDED IN CAPTURING IT—FROM ITS PICTURE IT WAS ESTIMATED TO BE 12 FEET HIGH, WITH TUSKS 11 FEET LONG AND COMPRISING *200 POUNDS OF IVORY*

THE FIRST COOK BOOK

ARCHESTRATUS of GELA, a Greek poet, PUBLISHED "The Art of Cooking" COMPRISING SEVERAL HUNDRED RECIPES IN RHYME *IN THE 4th CENTURY B.C.*

PIGEON NESTS

FOUND IN AN ABANDONED STEEL FOUNDRY WERE MADE ENTIRELY OF STRIPS OF *STEEL, BRASS, COPPER AND ALUMINUM*

A PAPER MODEL

OF THE DECEASED'S HOUSE IS CREMATED WITH THE BODY AT CHINESE FUNERALS TO ASSURE THE SOUL A FAMILIAR DWELLING

THE KANGAROO RAT WILL DIE UNLESS IT TAKES FREQUENT DUST-BATHS

JOHANN BERNARDUS HEINEMANN AND GEORG WILHELM TILL SERVED SUCCESSIVELY AS PASTORS of the church in Wolfershausen, Germany BOTH HAD THE SAME BIRTHDAY—EACH WAS 32 YEARS OF AGE AT HIS INAUGURATION —BOTH SERVED EXACTLY 22 YEARS AND EACH DIED ON A FRIDAY—ON HIS 54th BIRTHDAY

FIG WITH A NATURAL MARKING OF THE NUMERAL 7

THE AIRBORNE STEEPLE Honfleur, France IT WAS BLOWN FROM ITS CHURCH TO THE ROOF OF THE BELLRINGER'S HOUSE ACROSS THE STREET WHERE IT HAS REMAINED FOR MORE THAN 500 YEARS

DR. R.C. SPANGLER
of Morgantown, W.Va.,
PLAYED 83 HOLES OF GOLF
AND SCORED 83 ON ONE
OF THE 18-HOLE ROUNDS
ON *HIS 83d BIRTHDAY*

PREDICTIONS
ARE MADE BY NATIVES
OF THE CAMEROONS, AFRICA,
USING THE BURROWS OF
NATIVE GIANT SPIDERS—
THE NATIVES SCATTER LEAVES
OVER 11 RIBBONS AROUND THE
BURROW AND THE NEXT MORNING
BASE THEIR PROPHECIES ON
THE WAY THE SPIDER HAS
REARRANGED THE LEAVES

JEAN-BAPTISTE MAQUINAZ
A FAMOUS ALPINE MOUNTAIN GUIDE
LOST ALL 10 TOES AND THE
SOLES OF BOTH FEET AFTER
THEY FROZE IN 1893 — YET
HE CONTINUED TO LEAD ALPINE
CLIMBS FOR ANOTHER 30 YEARS

THE DESERT NIGHT LIZARD
(Xantusia)
TO DISTRACT AN ATTACKER
SHEDS ITS TAIL

THE BEE ORCHID HAS A BLOOM SHAPED *AMAZINGLY LIKE A BEE*

THE **BIRTHMARK** THAT WAS WORTH $11,200,000,000

HO SHEN A PRIVATE IN THE CHINESE ARMY WAS MADE PRIME MINISTER AND GIVEN A FORTUNE ESTIMATED AT $11,200,000,000 BY EMPEROR CHIEN LUNG IN 1776 BECAUSE OF A RED BIRTHMARK ON HO SHEN'S NECK

MA CHIA, THE EMPEROR'S FAVORITE CONCUBINE, HAD A SIMILAR MARK—AND THE RULER THOUGHT HO SHEN WAS A REINCARNATION OF MA CHIA

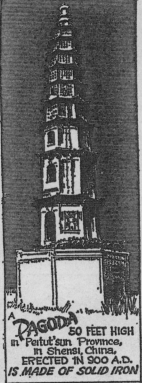

A **PAGODA** 50 FEET HIGH IN Peitut'sun Province, in Shensi, China, ERECTED IN 900 A.D. *IS MADE OF SOLID IRON*

A *GRAVE* in Warringal Cemetery, Melbourne, Australia, IS MARKED BY 2 BEER BARRELS —AND BEARS THE EPITAPH: GOD HELP THE RICH THE POOR HAVE LESS TO CARRY

TERMITE NESTS OFTEN RESEMBLE A *HUGE MUSHROOM*

THE MAN WHO COULD NOT ESCAPE HIS FATE

BIBARS JASHENGIR TOLD THAT HE MUST BECOME SULTAN OF EGYPT OR DIE BY STRANGULATION, ACCEPTED THE CROWN ON APRIL 5, 1309— ONLY 10 MONTHS LATER HE WAS DEFEATED IN BATTLE —AND EXECUTED BY STRANGLING

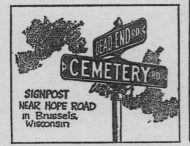

SIGNPOST NEAR HOPE ROAD in Brussels, Wisconsin

1,500 OASES

in the Sahara Desert OF A TOTAL OF 2,000 OASES IN THE AREA *WERE ARTIFICIALLY CREATED—* THEY COMPRISE IRRIGATED VALLEYS IN WHICH PALM TREES WERE PLANTED TO PROVIDE SHADE

AN **ABORIGINE WIDOW** of the River Murray Tribe of Australia MUST MOURN HER DEAD HUSBAND FOR 3 MONTHS ADDING AN ADDITIONAL LAYER OF CLAY TO HER HEAD EACH DAY AT THE END OF THE MOURNING PERIOD A 14-POUND COATING OF CLAY AND ALL HER HAIR ARE REMOVED TOGETHER AND PLACED IN THE HUSBAND'S GRAVE -TO ASSURE HIM HIS WIDOW HAS TRULY MOURNED HIM

MATT WARNER (1864-1938) of Utah AFTER SPENDING 3 YEARS IN PRISON FOR MANSLAUGHTER AND A CAREER AS A BANK ROBBER AND CATTLE RUSTLER SERVED THE LAST 38 YEARS OF HIS LIFE AS A DEPUTY SHERIFF, DETECTIVE, POLICEMAN AND JUSTICE OF THE PEACE

THE **WILLIAMS-TAUZIN HOUSE** in Natchitoches, La., BUILT IN 1776 WITHOUT NAILS, CONSIDERED VIRTUALLY INDESTRUCTIBLE BECAUSE ITS WALLS CONSIST OF ADOBE MIXED WITH DEER HIDES

THE FIRST DICE USED IN GAMBLING WERE ACTUALLY THE ANKLE BONES OF SHEEP

BRITISH SOLDIERS
in India and the Colonies
FOR YEARS STAGED
WRESTLING MATCHES
ON HORSEBACK

GUILLEMOT EGGS
ARE OFTEN HATCHED
*BY BEING SAT
UPON BY THE
MALE AND FEMALE
SIMULTANEOUSLY*

THE **CLARENDON BUILDING**
in Oxford, England,
*BUILT WITH THE PROFITS OF ONE
BOOK PUBLISHED IN 1707*

THE **WILD** GEESE
OF THE
FALKLAND ISLANDS
*HAVE A PRICE
ON THEIR BEAKS*
THE AUTHORITIES
PAY FOR EACH
GOOSE KILLED
BECAUSE A SINGLE
GOOSE CAN EAT
AS MUCH GRASS
AS A SHEEP

WANTED
DEAD OR ALIVE

CLAUDE GILLOT
(1673-1722) famed French painter
AFTER TAKING AS A PUPIL A
YOUNG NOVICE NAMED WATTEAU
QUIT PAINTING AND SWITCHED TO
ENGRAVING BECAUSE HE REALIZED
AFTER WORKING ONLY A FEW
MONTHS WITH WATTEAU THAT
*HE COULD NEVER EQUAL THE
MASTERY OF HIS STUDENT*

JAMES TAIT
A SCOTTISH RECLUSE
WHO SHARED A LONELY CABIN
WITH HIS MOTHER FOR 70 YEARS
*CONTINUED TO SET A PLACE FOR
HER AT EVERY MEAL FOR 25
YEARS AFTER HER DEATH*

A GIRL in the Shona Tribe
of Rhodesia
MUST APPROACH HER HUSBAND
OR FATHER *ON HER KNEES*

THE REPUBLICAN PRESIDENTIAL TICKET OF 1892

WITH BENJAMIN HARRISON *AND* WHITELAW REID THE
THE CANDIDATE FOR PRESIDENT NOMINEE FOR VICE PRESIDENT
IS THE ONLY ONE IN AMERICAN HISTORY IN WHICH
BOTH CANDIDATES WERE GRADUATES OF THE SAME UNIVERSITY
THEY ATTENDED MIAMI UNIVERSITY OF OHIO

BENJAMIN F. BUTLER (1795-1858)
WAS THE ONLY MAN IN U.S. HISTORY
TO SERVE IN 2 CABINET POSTS
SIMULTANEOUSLY —
FOR 10 MONTHS IN 1836 AND 1837
HE WAS ATTORNEY GENERAL AND
ALSO SECRETARY OF WAR

TREE GROWING
IN THE SHAPE
OF A WITCH

NANCY PERRIAM
(1767-1865) of Exmouth England,
WHO REFUSED TO BE SEPARATED
FROM HER SAILOR HUSBAND,
SERVED VALIANTLY AS A POWDER
MONKEY ON THE ENGLISH
WARSHIPS CRESCENT AND ORION
*FIGHTING WITH ADMIRAL NELSON
IN MANY NAVAL BATTLES*
SHE RETIRED IN 1798 AND
RECEIVED A NAVY PENSION
FOR 67 YEARS

THE SUNDEW PLANT
HAS HAIRS ON ITS
LEAVES WHICH
GLISTEN IN THE SUN
LIKE DROPS OF DEW,
LURING THIRSTY
INSECTS WHICH THE
*PLANT SMOTHERS
AND DEVOURS*

PAOLO ALBONI
FAMED ITALIAN LANDSCAPE PAINTER
WHO LOST THE USE OF HIS RIGHT
HAND AS A RESULT OF A STROKE
*LEARNED TO PAINT WITH EQUAL
MASTERY WITH HIS LEFT HAND*

RELIGIOUS STATUES of the Guatemalan Indians ARE MADE OF INDIAN CORN DOUGH - BUT THE HEADS ARE COVERED *WITH HUMAN HAIR*

THE FORTUNE-TELLING HATS OF THE TARAHUMARES

THE TARAHUMARE INDIANS of Mexico DANCE WITH WOODEN HATS, BEARING LONG STREAMERS, WHIRLING UNTIL THEY COLLAPSE - AT WHICH TIME TRIBAL SOOTH-SAYERS PREDICT FUTURE EVENTS' BY THE DIRECTIONS IN WHICH THE VARIOUS DANCERS FALL

THE HANGING HOUSES of TARAZONA (Spain) HOMES BUILT ON A 600-YEAR-OLD CITY WALL *WITH THEIR ROOMS ACTUALLY CAVES EXCAVATED FROM THE ROCK*

POR'ANIE? — JLURMISRE!

THE PRIMITIVE LAPPS of Norway and Sweden HAVE 20 DIFFERENT WORDS FOR "ICE" AND 40 EXPRESSIONS FOR "SNOW"

A DWELLING OF THE Somba Tribe, Africa, REVEALS BY THE NUMBER OF ITS TURRETS HOW MANY OF THE FAMILY'S CHILDREN ARE AVAILABLE FOR MARRIAGE A TURRET ROOM IS BUILT AS SOON AS A CHILD REACHES ADOLESCENCE AND IS TORN DOWN WHEN ITS OCCUPANT MARRIES

ACTORS in ancient Rome WHEN THEY DIED ALWAYS WERE BURIED WEARING THE MASKS OF THEIR STAGE ROLES THIS WAS TO MAKE CERTAIN THEY WOULD BE JUDGED IN THE HEREAFTER BY THEIR ACTING ABILITY RATHER THAN THEIR PRIVATE CONDUCT

WOODEN LOCKS ARE STILL USED ON DOORS IN SOUTHERN ARABIA - UNCHANGED SINCE THEY WERE FIRST USED IN ANCIENT TIMES

SHRINES in Ceylon FOR THE CONVENIENCE OF TRAVELERS ARE LOCATED AMONG THE ROOTS OF SACRED BANYAN TREES

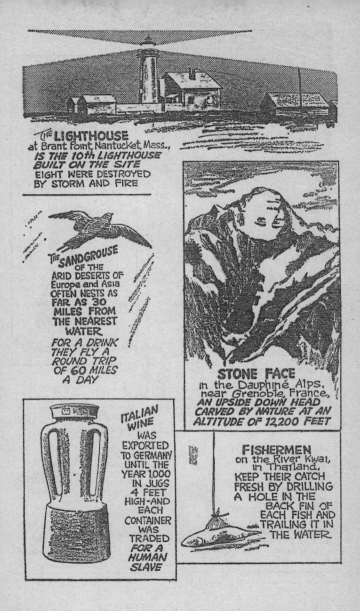

THE **LIGHTHOUSE**
at Brant Point, Nantucket, Mass.,
*IS THE 10th LIGHTHOUSE
BUILT ON THE SITE*
EIGHT WERE DESTROYED
BY STORM AND FIRE

THE **SANDGROUSE**
OF THE
ARID DESERTS OF
Europe and Asia
OFTEN NESTS AS
FAR AS 30
MILES FROM
THE NEAREST
WATER
*FOR A DRINK
THEY FLY A
ROUND TRIP
OF 60 MILES
A DAY*

STONE FACE
in the Dauphiné Alps,
near Grenoble, France,
*AN UPSIDE DOWN HEAD
CARVED BY NATURE AT AN
ALTITUDE OF 12,200 FEET*

ITALIAN WINE
WAS
EXPORTED
TO GERMANY
UNTIL THE
YEAR 1,000
IN JUGS
4 FEET
HIGH–AND
EACH
CONTAINER
WAS
TRADED
*FOR A
HUMAN
SLAVE*

FISHERMEN
on the River Kwai,
in Thailand,
KEEP THEIR CATCH
FRESH BY DRILLING
A HOLE IN THE
BACK FIN OF
EACH FISH AND
TRAILING IT IN
THE WATER

ANTONIO MORELLI
(1739-1814) THE OPERA SINGER
WAS ONLY 16 YEARS OF AGE WHEN HE
WAS BURIED FOR A WEEK UNDER A
DEMOLISHED CHURCH BY THE GREAT
EARTHQUAKE OF NOV. 1755, in Lisbon, Portugal
-YET HIS HAIR TURNED SNOW WHITE

THE
**BEGGING
DOG**
NATURAL
COAL
FORMATION
in Halle on
the Saale,
Germany,
*THAT LOOKS
LIKE A
SITTING
DOG*

THE PHRASE
"A PARTING SHOT"
ORIGINALLY WAS
"A PARTHIAN SHOT"
-A BACKWARD SHOT
WITH BOW AND
ARROW BY WHICH
THE PARTHIANS OF
ASIA KILLED THEIR
ENEMIES AFTER
HAVING PRETENDED
TO FLEE

from an old print

COUNT ANTON GÜNTHER
ruler of Oldenburg
AS A JEST PROPOSED TO THE INFANT PRINCESS
SOPHIA OF HOLSTEIN AT HER BAPTISM
HE MARRIED THE PRINCESS 18 YEARS LATER

ARCTIC LAND
near Spitzbergen, Norway,
AS THE RESULT OF ALTERNATE
FREEZING AND THAWING
*OFTEN FORMS AMAZING
SYMMETRICAL SECTIONS
-EACH SEPARATED BY A
BORDER OF STONES*

THE **JACKASS PENGUIN**
of the
Cape,
South Africa,
BRAYS LIKE A DONKEY

DR. KARL von KUPFFER
a 20th century author of Estonia
BECAME SO ENAMORED OF OLIVER CROMWELL'S
PERIOD WHILE WRITING A BOOK ABOUT IT THAT
*HE ADOPTED THE 17TH CENTURY VAN DYKE,
HAIRDO, HAT, SHOES AND COMPLETE COSTUME*

THE FIRST FEMALE JURIST IN AMERICA
ESTHER HOBART MORRIS
A SUFFRAGETTE of South Pass City Wyoming, WAS APPOINTED JUSTICE OF THE PEACE 96 YEARS AGO

THE LARGEST SHIP MODEL IN THE WORLD
THE LAGODA, A HALF-SIZE REPLICA OF AN ACTUAL WHALING SHIP IN THE WHALING MUSEUM, NEW BEDFORD, MASS., IS 59 FEET LONG AND HAS A MAST 50 FEET HIGH

CESAR PHEBUS d'ALBRET (1614-1676)
MARSHAL OF FRANCE WAS FAMED FOR HIS FEARLESSNESS -YET THE SIGHT OF A BOAR'S HEAD SERVED ON A PLATTER AT DINNER ALWAYS MADE HIM FAINT

QUEEN ANNE of England CREATED A LANE IN ASHRIDGE PARK BY PLANTING 17 LIME TREES - EACH A MEMORIAL TO ONE OF HER CHILDREN, *ALL 17 OF WHOM DIED IN INFANCY*

AN *ELEPHANT'S SKIN* REPRESENTS 1/6 th OF ITS TOTAL WEIGHT

A **WIDOW** in Toro, Spain, *SEEKING A SECOND HUSBAND* WEAVES WHITE THREADS IN HER COIFFURE **TO ADVERTISE THAT SHE IS A WOMAN OF MEANS**

10 DIFFERENT SIGNS MEANING "WOMAN" ARE USED BY THE KEITA TRIBE OF AFRICA *- DEPENDING UPON HER AGE*

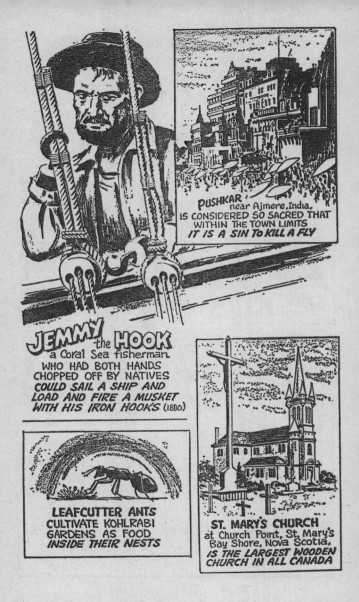

PUSHKAR near Ajmere, India, IS CONSIDERED SO SACRED THAT WITHIN THE TOWN LIMITS *IT IS A SIN TO KILL A FLY*

JEMMY the **HOOK** a Coral Sea fisherman WHO HAD BOTH HANDS CHOPPED OFF BY NATIVES *COULD SAIL A SHIP AND LOAD AND FIRE A MUSKET WITH HIS IRON HOOKS* (1880)

LEAFCUTTER ANTS CULTIVATE KOHLRABI GARDENS AS FOOD *INSIDE THEIR NESTS*

ST. MARY'S CHURCH at Church Point, St. Mary's Bay Shore, Nova Scotia, *IS THE LARGEST WOODEN CHURCH IN ALL CANADA*

KA·HE·TE·RAU·O·TE·RANGI
A MOTHER LIVING ON Kapiti, New Zealand, TO GET HELP WHEN THE ISLAND WAS ATTACKED *SWAM 7 MILES THROUGH THE ICE-COLD PACIFIC TO THE MAINLAND WITH HER 5-YEAR-OLD DAUGHTER ON HER BACK*

SHE HAD 20 MORE CHILDREN IN THE YEARS FOLLOWING THE SWIM WHICH MADE HER A NATIONAL HEROINE

SMALL HOUSES WERE BUILT AGAINST THE INSIDE OF THE TOWN WALL of Nördlingen, Germany, in the 17th century *TO HOUSE SOLDIERS IN TIME OF SIEGE*— IN PEACETIME CIVILIANS OCCUPIED THE HOUSES WITHOUT RENT - BUT THEY HAD TO BE READY TO VACATE AT A MOMENT'S NOTICE

MARGARET·PATRICIA HARCOURT
REFUSED BY THE WOMEN'S ROYAL NAVAL SERVICE OF ENGLAND BECAUSE OF A MALFORMED LEFT ARM, ENTERED A PRIVATE HOSPITAL AND HAD THE *ARM AMPUTATED* — FITTED WITH AN ARTIFICIAL ARM SHE WAS ACCEPTED BY THE WRENS AND PERFORMED DISTINGUISHED SERVICE

THE SPHINX
NATURAL ROCK FORMATION
Palm Valley, Queensland, Australia

MARY DUNN
of Bonne Terre, Missouri,
HAD A VOCABULARY OF
3,800 WORDS
A REPERTOIRE OF
100 SONGS
AND AN I.Q. OF 185—
45 POINTS ABOVE
THE GENIUS LEVEL—
AT THE AGE OF
28 MONTHS

A LARGE TREE
near Windhoek, Southwest Africa,
GROWING OUT OF A
TERMITES' NEST

THE FONT IN
THE CHAPEL OF
THE ROYAL AIR
FORCE TRAINING
COLLEGE IN
Cranwell, England
IS CONSTRUCTED
ENTIRELY FROM
AIRPLANE
ENGINES